WHAT THE HECK IS DBT?

THE SECRET TO UNDERSTANDING YOUR EMOTIONS AND COPING WITH YOUR ANXIETY THROUGH DIALECTICAL BEHAVIOR THERAPY SKILLS.

R.J. MILLER

CONTENTS

INTRODUCTION

"You can't calm the storm, so stop trying. What you can do is calm yourself. The storm will pass."

— TIMBER HAWKEYE

"Who would have thought life could be so interesting and fun! After so many years of suffering in silence and living in pain, I can now feel and enjoy life like everyone else!"

For many years, I couldn't appreciate simple things like the smell of coffee, birds chirping, watching the sun rise and set, and all the other amazing things nature has to offer. Instead, I was more engrossed in dealing with intense emotions.

Every day felt like I was dealing with the worst heartbreak as I was in a *"pain loop"* with no escape route.

On the outside, it may look like I had it all together; I worked in a fantastic organization, had great friends and incredible parents. However, no one knew the demons I battled inside. I felt pressured to be perfect. Whenever I didn't do well, I felt hopeless and overwhelmed with emotions. When my girlfriends broke up with me, I saw them as the problem. "Why can't they accept me for who I am?" "Why are they pretending to love me when they don't?" "Why can't this, why can't that…." I always asked myself so many "whys."

Even though I failed to admit it, I've had many up-and-down moments. I knew there was a problem with how I reacted to things, but I could not pinpoint what was wrong with me or how to improve myself and the situation.

I never spoke about how I truly felt and never thought I would. I was worried that it would make people avoid me. Since how I felt did not make sense to me, how would it make sense to others? Besides, I have never been a talker; I was used to bottling my feelings and getting angry at myself. I was a more "traditional man" who grew up in a family where men hardly talked about their feelings and weren't encouraged to speak up. Speaking up as a man may portray you as weak, and that's the last thing I wanted people to see me as. So, I joined the bandwagon and had to pay the price.

I continued hiding my feelings and thoughts until they started keeping me awake at night. I would lay sleepless in my bed and cry for hours. I would be so tired the next day at work and highly unproductive. I would feel cranky, and everything my boss said became annoying. Whenever friends complained about my actions, I would turn it against them and feel like they didn't know how to have a good time.

This continued until I started having issues at the one place I excelled; my job! I loved what I did but didn't know what to do because it seemed like a never-ending cycle. I was in a bad place and eventually left the job I loved. I was now ALONE!

Luckily for me, my parents intervened. However, it took weeks of convincing from them before I finally agreed to see a doctor. The doctor assessed and diagnosed me with Borderline Personality Disorder (BPD). I remember feeling scared and upset when I heard about BPD. The diagnosis was upsetting because I had difficulty accepting my "disordered personality." However, despite the harsh words and stigma attached to it, the diagnosis still brought me some relief. I finally understood what was happening to me and realized that there was a way out of the ditch I was rotting in.

Let me guess; you're experiencing something similar? You see yourself swinging from one extreme emotion to another within seconds, acting impulsive and recklessly, and suddenly bored with life. You find it difficult to cope with your fluctuating emotions, your brain is overworking, and you're full of guilt and fear. You've never felt like you're good enough, leading to panic and anxiety because you're afraid your emotional distress will push others away and you will be alone.

Perhaps, you see yourself drowning in these intense emotions with no help. You are tired of not knowing the cause of your emotional problems and feel you've lost control of your life. If you feel like you're on a conveyor belt, and the inevitable end is a giant grinder with no idea of how to stop the belt or get off it, then you aren't alone.

Many have similar experiences as you; it was happening to me, and I realized there was a way out of the ditch I was rotting in.

Many expectations come with understanding and managing your emotions, but this isn't an inborn skill; you get to learn it. The situations I've described above should be easily fixed without much hassle. However, it becomes even more frustrating and self-loathing when you don't know where to start or how to go about it.

I understand that you're tired of where your life is right now, you've been seeking help, and you desperately want to see changes. You want to live like everyone else, do things and enjoy life like them.

So, what do you do? How do you escape this tunnel of deep pain and break free from this horror?

First, you need to understand that you're the only one responsible for your life, and only you can change it. This is the turning point. All the emotional turmoil you've experienced can change if you commit to helping yourself.

Although I can't promise that there's a magic wand that I can wave and take away your pain instantly, I can guarantee that this book will introduce you to Dialectical Behavior Therapy (DBT) in a simplified way.

DBT is a research-based psychotherapy that has been proven effective in helping people suffering from anxiety, depression, Borderline Personality Disorder (BPD), eating disorders, and substance abuse find relief. This evidence-based therapy strengthens your ability to handle distress without acting destructively or losing control. You will first accept your feelings as a valid part of your experience, build a tolerance to distress, and effectively regulate your emotions.

With DBT, you can understand and manage your fluctuating emotions, overcome impulsive behaviors, improve your self-awareness, and effectively deal with relationship issues you may have. DBT aims to help you control your emotions and be the best version of yourself!

The most rewarding thing about DBT is knowing that having intense feelings doesn't mean you should act on them; you have a choice on how to act in difficult situations. You need to acknowledge the emotions and be non-judgmental about them.

For many years, I was scared of letting people know how I felt or giving an explanation for my constant withdrawal from people. However, looking back now and considering the many years of living in pain, I am glad I am writing this book. This book will serve as a medium to share my experience and help other people with similar experiences as I find relief.

Before I got introduced to DBT, I tried traditional therapy without much luck. I knew I had to try something more hands-on that I could practice daily with quicker results rather than talking to someone weekly. No doubt, talk therapy also has its benefits. But, I wanted something I could do independently and get life-changing results.

I went online, researched DBT, and printed a heap of information on it. I highlighted essential lines on each page, which suddenly all made sense to me! Everything I bottled up that didn't make sense, that I couldn't put my fingers on, and that I couldn't explain to others were on those pages.

I used what I learned and started journaling the results of various DBT practices. My life completely changed within six months of applying DBT skills and tools! I was able to manage my stress and thoughts more effectively.

Even though it took me six months to see a significant difference, DBT is a lifetime practice that shouldn't be a headache or a chore. It's about continuously learning more about yourself and improving daily. The DBT skills I've learned have positively impacted every area of my life, career, family and friends, and meaningful relationships. Thanks to DBT, I can now manage my emotions successfully, something that not everyone can do, and it's something I am very proud of.

This book has been written to help you better understand the fundamentals of DBT and teach you how to use DBT skills to live in the present, tolerate distress, effectively manage your relationships, regulate your emotions, and improve your life. In addition, it offers easy and fun exercises to engage in and control your emotions.

I've written this book because I've been there. I've experienced chronic pain and felt broken and depressed. I've been aggressive over nothing, totally lost it when I shouldn't of, felt various discomforting emotions, and even had suicidal tendencies. I got tired of living that way and finally accepted that I needed help.

Acceptance was my first step to recovery, and from there, other measures followed. Trust me, it wasn't easy at first because I made many mistakes. But, I tested all I learned and sieved through to know strategies that work and those that don't.

For some time, I've had an enormous passion for this subject, and I want to help as many people struggling with their emotions as possible. What you will learn in the following chapters is a well-crafted and careful collection of my personal experience and information from experts in the field.

Even though it will be challenging initially, I know you will get through it. With this book, the ride ahead will be smoother. Your efforts will be worth it, and you will be confident knowing that you now have access to tools that will make a significant difference in your life. Always remember that you deserve to be happy and live a peaceful life.

Are you ready to break free from the shackles of your emotions, challenge your assumptions, react more rationally to situations, and learn to live in the present moment peacefully?

Let's get started as we uncover everything you need to know about the fundamentals of DBT in the first chapter.

1

THE FUNDAMENTALS OF DIALECTICAL BEHAVIOR THERAPY

"W*hat exactly is this therapy?"*

This was me asking my therapist about DBT when he suggested it. He hasn't practiced it himself, but he had opinions about it. Some of his perspectives suggested that DBT is a helpful therapy that provides skills for patients to practice. These skills allow you to connect with your spiritual side since it's practical and not difficult to understand and engage in. Also, the group component of DBT lets you see how others are using it and gives you hope that you can do it too. His explanation calmed me a bit, even if I still felt reluctant.

For many people unfamiliar with DBT, this concept may initially sound strange. Some may assume it is a complicated therapy and, like me, feel reluctant to try it. This chapter aims to set the record straight by clearly explaining what DBT entails, starting with its effectiveness in helping people suffering from a wide range of issues such as low self-image, impulsivity, and anger. Below, I will also introduce the four areas of DBT and why every human deserves a life worth living.

With so many therapies, it becomes hard to know one from another and know the best option for you. So, it's crucial that you know more about this therapy before embarking on this journey.

First, let's start by discussing what DBT is.

What Is DBT?

DBT is a cognitive-behavioral treatment initially developed to treat suicide patients diagnosed with BPD. This science-backed therapy has become a gold standard psychological treatment for treating other disorders, including anxiety, depression, eating disorders, substance abuse, post-traumatic stress disorder (PTSD), and self-harm.

DBT is a practical treatment that gives access to skills needed to handle the "extreme" ups and downs of your emotions. It encourages you to face your uncomfortable feelings and learn to manage them instead of avoiding them. With DBT, you will become aware of what's going on in your body; that way, you can be more in control of your brain.

DBT aims to help people live in and enjoy the moment while accessing healthier ways to cope with stress. While cognitive behavioral therapy (CBT) aims to identify and change unhelpful thoughts, DBT teaches skills to manage overwhelming and painful emotions. It also provides strategies to reduce conflicts in relationships.

Psychologist Marsha Linehan originally created DBT to treat individuals with chronic suicide cases who also suffer from BPD (borderline personality disorder). However, this treatment seems to be gaining more attention and popularity daily. As a result, more people are now flexible in adopting this treatment.

The first word, "dialectical," explains the three core beliefs of this philosophy:

- Change is constant and inevitable.
- Opposites can be united to get closer to the truth.
- Everything is interconnected.

This means that two seemingly opposites can be accurate at the same time.

For example, even though I was being shitty to people around me before I got diagnosed with BPD, I still had my good sides. I truly cared about my family and friends and always wanted the best for them. I try to show it whenever I am not experiencing my down moments. So, being a jerk and, at the same time, a caring guy are two opposing facts that are true at the same time.

In DBT, people are taught two opposite strategies (acceptance and change), which means they must make positive changes to manage their emotions and live peacefully.

The History Behind DBT

The founder of DBT, Dr. Marsha Linehan, started researching new alternatives to treat suicidal thoughts in the 70s after her own struggles with mental health. The psychologist knew nothing about BPD at that time but later got to know much about it.

Years ago, Linehan revealed in the New York Times that she struggled with mental illness in her late teens. After overcoming the struggles, she developed a particular interest in helping others who were also struggling with the same issue. In her words, she wanted to "get them out of hell."

When Linehan started working with suicidal patients in the 70s, she realized it was easy to get grant money since she was the only one carrying out randomized controlled trials with suicidal patients. Her team would request that the hospital in the area send the most severe cases of suicide and self-harm to them. She then tried to cure them with behavioral therapy.

When using behaviorism, the patients would respond feeling like they were the problem. This isn't surprising because behaviorism entails a model of change. So, when she gave feedback on how they could change and improve their symptoms, they took it wrongly and assumed she said it was their fault. Their responses were along the line of: "What are you saying? How is this my fault? What about my kids? My spouse? My employer? And the environment I live in? Aren't these making it difficult for me to get better? So how is it my fault?

Based on the patient's response, using only behavioral therapy wasn't enough. The behaviorism approach was already popular during this time, but the humanistic approach also dominated. So, she felt that trying the humanistic approach should be worth it.

Since behaviorism is known for being cut, dry, and sterile, Linehan was willing to consider the other approach – humanism. According to her, it should be a more appropriate stance, and that was how she tried it! But unfortunately, it didn't go as planned either.

Looking at both approaches – humanism, and behaviorism as being at the end of the continuum, they seemed like opposites. So Linehan went from one end to another and found that both approaches didn't give the result she expected.

While researching what would work, Linehan and her team watched through a one-way mirror where they could see patients and study them without being seen. She would study the patients, try out her ideas, and take notes. She later found that certain things she does or tells the patients upset them while other things were more regulating. This discovery wasn't something different or a third theory; it was like a blend of behaviorism and humanism. So, instead of choosing a side and moving back and forth between the concepts, Linehan decided to stay in the fulcrum of both. Dialectics was what seemed to be the balance of the two opposite theories. Linehan and her team were able to see positive results with a bit of practice and patience. Then, as the 90s came around, DBT became a therapeutic choice for BPD.

The origin of DBT involves a non-pejorative stance. Rather than call the patients manipulative or refer to them as the problem, DBT was the approach that equals between client and therapist. This balance she got was also influenced by her Zen training.

You'll notice a similarity if studying DBT and Zen behavior therapy closely. During training, Linehan found many principles she learned in Zen, and her meditation could be applied to her patients to achieve positive results.

HOW DBT DIFFERS FROM OTHER THERAPIES

Despite having basic similarities, DBT and CBT aren't the same. While some patients respond to DBT better, others find that CBT works better for them. This is because the main focus of CBT is on rational thinking, while DBT does the same but focuses more on emotions.

When you understand the definition of DBT, you can quickly know how it differs from other therapies. DBT aims to help patients balance their emotions and improve their behavioral patterns. It starts with identifying these emotions and thought patterns leading to the distress you're experiencing. Then it teaches you how to use the thoughts with healthier ideas to give a more beneficial result. Instead of changing your thoughts and behaviors entirely, DBT suggests that you should adopt a more balanced worldview.

Although some people learn DBT skills independently. (practicing on their own without the help of a therapist) DBT is usually taught in a group setting comprising of four sessions.

CBT focuses on feelings, thoughts, and behaviors as they influence each other. When you apply CBT, you will be learning to see when your thoughts are becoming an issue, and you can then redirect your thoughts using CBT techniques.

No doubt, DBT recognizes dangers just as CBT does. Still, it focuses more on emotions, being mindful, and accepting that pain is part of the human experience. With this acknowledgment, you will feel safer managing difficult emotions, and you can regulate your destructive behaviors more.

Let's quickly discuss some points that reveal how DBT differs from CBT.

Philosophies: The approach of both DBT and CBT differs. DBT focuses on how you interact with yourself and others, using mindfulness philosophies to help you accept yourself and your environment. CBT, on the other hand, is more logic focused as it encourages you to use critical thinking to find healthier ways to think and behave.

Goals: CBT is more goal-oriented than DBT. DBT does have goals. However, it isn't as direct and firm as CBT. While DBT focuses on social and emotional aspects, CBT focuses on your behaviors. The idea behind DBT is to help you find a way to accept yourself, manage your emotions effectively, and regulate the unhelpful behaviors you may have.

Types of Sessions: DBT sessions last longer than CBT. While CBT lasts for a few weeks, a DBT session is usually a months-long process. DBT also involves a group therapy component where you have a safe and supportive environment to practice skills like interpersonal communication.

Uses: Since DBT focuses on regulating intense emotions and CBT focuses on changing unhelpful thoughts, both therapies have different uses. DBT is clinically proven effective in treating BPD, self-harm, eating disorders, emotional dysregulation, anger, substance use disorders, anxiety, and depression. CBT is effective for treating depression, anxiety, Post-Traumatic Stress Disorder (PTSD), phobia, Obsessive

Compulsive Disorders (OCD), and Generalized Anxiety Disorders (GAD).

WHAT CAN DBT HELP TREAT

Now that you know how DBT differs from other therapies, especially CBT, we can explore how you can benefit from this therapy.

Even though Masha Linehan initially developed DBT to treat BPD, the techniques have proven to be effective in treating other mental health conditions such as bipolar disorder, depression, anxiety, PTSD, GAD, attention deficit hyperactivity disorder (ADHD), substance use disorders, and eating disorders.

Besides the mental conditions, DBT can help people cope with extreme stress, intense emotions, relationship difficulties, manage challenging situations, suicidal ideation, and self-injurious behavior.

Other notable areas that DBT can be helpful in include:

- Ability to make healthier choices.
- Communication skills.
- Moving toward a solution instead of problems.
- Ability to view things from different perspectives.
- Knowing more about your values and goals.
- Healthier thinking patterns.
- Improved awareness of negative thoughts.

- Have more significant insights into your life.
- Develop skills to face challenges in the present and future.
- Have coping strategies to manage distress.

THE CORE PRINCIPLES OF DBT

DBT aims to reduce the emotional distress that may impact your well-being and how you interact with your environment. It focuses on skills training that includes mindfulness, distress tolerance, emotion regulation, and interpersonal effectiveness. These are the four main components of DBT that, when used right, promises to free you from the shackles of anxiety, and you can go ahead and live your best life! Now, let me explain the component to give you a better understanding.

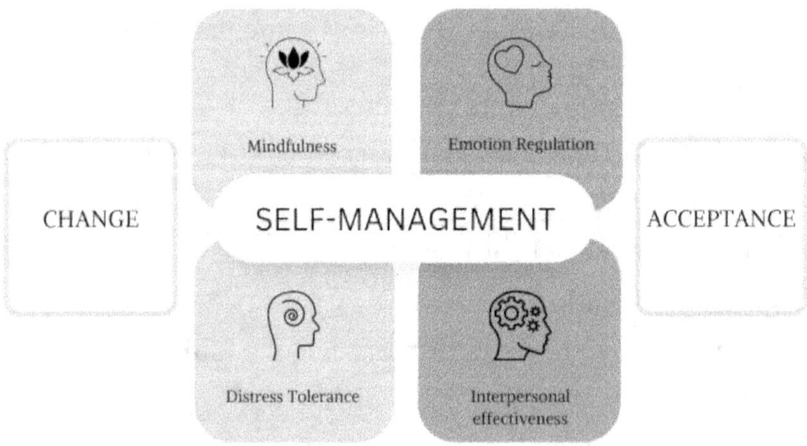

Mindfulness

When dealing with anxiety, it's easy to get worried about what has happened in the past and what will happen in the future. However, with mindfulness skills, you can learn to live in the present and accept what is happening in the present rather than dwell in the past, try not to predict the future, and accept your feelings and thoughts without judgment. Same thing with depression; the condition makes one get stuck in the past, reflecting on what could've or should've happened.

In DBT, mindfulness is grouped into the "how" and "what" skills. The "how" skills teach you to be mindful by taking effective actions while accepting aspects of yourself through radical acceptance, balancing your emotions rationally, and overcoming doubts and restlessness that may be hindering a mindful state. On the other hand, the "what" skills encourage you to focus on your present, emotions, thoughts, and sensations and learn how to separate your emotions from thoughts.

Distress tolerance

When you go through tough times, and you find it challenging to navigate, you can use healthier coping skills like distress tolerance to cope rather than destructive coping skills. Using coping skills such as self-isolating, angry outbursts, avoidance, self-harm, and substance abuse will only complicate issues and won't help. However, with distress tolerance, you can distract yourself until you feel calmer, more relaxed, and feel at peace. This means changing the moment regardless of the challenges and comparing the pros and cons of the available coping strategies.

Emotion regulation

Remember those times when you felt trapped in your emotions, and you couldn't escape them? Where you felt helpless, and nothing seemed to help. With emotion regulation, you can bring all those problematic emotions under your control, regardless of how overwhelming they feel.

As the name suggests, emotion regulation aims to regulate your emotions to prevent them from impacting your thoughts and behaviors. This skill focuses on a few goals: to reduce your emotional vulnerability, understand your emotions, reduce emotional suffering, solve problems in helpful ways, and overcome barriers to emotions that have positive effects.

In addition, with emotion regulation, you can learn to deal with primary emotional reactions that may lead to distressing secondary emotions. For example, anger is a primary emotion that can lead to feelings of guilt, worthlessness, and depression.

Interpersonal effectiveness

Remember how you felt when you had those rapid mood swings and intense emotions? How easy was it for you to move on and relate with others? I am guessing it was difficult. The goal of interpersonal effectiveness is that it helps you to clearly define what you want from how you feel.

When you master this DBT skill, you can confidently ask others about their needs and say "no" when the need arises. You will do these while maintaining self-respect and healthy boundaries with them. Asking questions and asserting one's self in a conversation is essential since you aren't a mind reader and shouldn't be assuming their needs. Assumptions can lead to wrong beliefs.

Interpersonal effectiveness aims to build healthy relationships with others by combining listening skills, social skills, assertiveness training, and setting clear boundaries to stay true to your values. The aim is to learn how to ask what you want the right way and take the necessary steps to get them, build self-respect, and learn how to walk through conflicts more effectively.

When you use these four skills of DBT, they allow you to go into the world and live the healthier, more meaningful, and realistic life you've longed for. In addition, each of the skills discussed strengthens and increases your chance of success as you navigate life.

I believe you now have a solid understanding of DBT and how it can help you regulate painful emotions. Although it takes a little practice, the benefits are very well documented. It's time to discuss one of the essential DBT skills – mindfulness.

See you in the next chapter!

2

MINDFULNESS AND ITS SIGNIFICANCE IN DBT

Society is known for taking something old and reinventing it, and a critical DBT skill – mindfulness isn't left out. Mindfulness is an ancient practice that was reinvented with the help of science. However, even before the involvement of science, this practice has been prevalent, and the reason isn't far from the many benefits it possesses.

When I first learned about DBT, I was surprised to know that mindfulness, a practice my closest friend, Ray, had always encouraged me to practice, was a core therapy skill that would end my misery.

Ray was born into a family that encouraged practicing mindfulness daily to maintain a stress-free and peaceful existence. I remember dismissing it when he suggested that I stay mindful of the present rather than worry about the past and future. I assumed the practice was religious or spiritual, and I wasn't down for that. However, I better understood mindfulness after my diagnosis with BPD. Over time, I realized that Ray had been right all along!

Mindfulness is at the heart of DBT as all skills learned through individual or group training start with it. This ancient act is vital in regulating emotions, getting through a crisis without worsening, and resolving interpersonal conflicts. This is because, without mindfulness, it is almost impossible to change the long-standing patterns of thoughts and actions.

To truly capture what mindfulness entails, we will take a brief look at its history, so you know it's not some hippie movement or the latest buzzword. In addition, there will be mention of certain studies to back its effectiveness and the basics of practicing it, including some guided meditation if you're beginning your mindfulness journey.

Just How Old Is Mindfulness

Mindfulness is linked as far back as 2500 years ago. Its origin is rooted in different religious and secular traditions, including Christianity, Hinduism, Islam, and Buddhism, before the interference of modern material practices.

Mindfulness in Hinduism

The history of mindfulness first links with the yogic practices of the Hindu people. This is between 2300 BC and 1500

BC, in Indus Valley, close to modern-day Pakistan. The Hindu scriptures reference acceptance, meditations, and silence; all these are vital elements of modern mindfulness that we practice today. Mindfulness is used as a preparatory practice for raja yoga in Hinduism. With it, you can attain a higher state of consciousness called "Dhyāna" which means contemplation in Hinduism. This exercise is practiced during yoga and aims to attain "Samadhi," which means a meditative state of consciousness. When doing this, your mind will remain and stick to the object of attention. You will gently observe what's happening internally and externally without being lost.

Same thing with the Sanskrit term "Smriti," which means remembering. The aim is to remember to be present in the relationship between yourself and the objects of your awareness.

Mindfulness in Buddhism

Buddhism has been around since 400-500 BC and was founded by Siddhārtha Gautama, the Buddha. Buddhists use meditation to ensure a state of ultimate consciousness, allowing personal attunement with a higher purpose in life. In Buddhism, mindfulness is taught as a way of giving enlightenment.

Sati, the first factor of the Seven Factors of Enlightenment in Buddhism, means mindfulness or remembering to be aware of something. This is a spiritual faculty that's an essential part of Buddhism. To get to the omniscient transcendental wisdom, Buddhists use mindfulness. So to them, it's necessary to be present when engaged in daily activities such as sitting, walking, eating, or working.

Mindful practices in Christianity and Islam

The history of mindfulness goes beyond different practices, even though Hinduism and Buddhism significantly influenced it. Mindfulness also has its roots in Islam, Judaism, and Christianity.

If you're familiar with Christianity, you might have heard the story of Jesus speaking about the "innermost I am." This entails the essence of the identity of every human – every life form. Certain Christian mystics have called this the "Christ within." Another instance is Brother Lawrence of the Resurrection, who served as a lay brother in a Carmelite monastery in Paris. He was known for always emphasizing being aware of the "Holy Spirit" when practicing in the presence of God.

The traces of mindfulness can also be seen in "Muraqabah." This is a Sufi meditation in Islam. Muraqabah aims to uplift the mind, heart, and body into peace, wellness, and happiness, which is the same thing mindfulness does. Through this practice, a person can watch over their heart and have an insight into the heart's relation with their creator and surroundings. In other words, it encourages continuous awareness.

Finally, even though you don't need to have a religious faith to practice mindfulness, it is still important to respect the origin of the important practice.

HOW MINDFULNESS GOT ITS LATEST REVIVAL

Mindfulness was recently introduced to the West in the 70s by Dr. Jon Kabat-Zinn. He taught mindfulness in both academic and medical contexts. Besides teaching mindfulness, he is the founder of the Center for Mindfulness at the University of Massachusetts Medical School. Kaba-Zinn describes mindfulness as "a means of paying attention in a particular way; on purpose, in the present moment, and nonjudgmentally." Even though it wasn't pointed out, his work is rooted in the Buddhist meditation practice.

Other notable people that brought mindfulness practices to the West are Sharon Salzberg, Jack Kornfield, and Joseph Goldstein. They founded the Insight Meditation Society (IMS) in 1975. At almost the same time, Marsha Linehan, the creator of DBT, got curious and wanted to know how helpful mindfulness is to people who were suicidal and had severe emotion dysregulation. So she translated what she learned from Zen principles into skills that aim to increase emotional control and attention.

Since then, mindfulness has been introduced to many institutions, including medical institutions, schools, sports, and wellness.

The latest revival of mindfulness was born after Dr. Jon Kabat-Zinn developed a stress-reduction program in the 1970s. The Mindfulness-Based Stress Reduction (MBSR) program is an 8-week program used in prisons, schools, and various industries, including politics, finance, and professional sports. An article published in time's magazine, *The Mindful Revolution, revealed that mindfulness got popularized, and thousands of MBSR instructors* started teaching mindfulness in over 30 countries. The widespread application and success of MBSR sparked what we know as "The Mindfulness Movement."

Even though there have been different forms of practicing mindfulness over the years, the purpose of this ancient practice has remained the same – to end pain and suffering. In addition, we owe most of the current wave of mindfulness therapies, exercises, and coaching we are witnessing to Kabat-Zinn's stress reduction program.

The effectiveness of MBSR in enhancing one's overall well-being and lowering stress has been supported by much scientific research. Among many is a study where the effectiveness of MBSR was implemented in a community setting as a self-paid course. The study, which included 115 randomized controlled trials (RCTs), suggests that MBSR has beneficial effects on anxiety, depression, stress, quality of life, physical functioning, and other conditions such as chronic pain, cancer, and cardiovascular (Juul et al., 2018).

Kabat-Zinn revealed that MBSR is based on Vipassana. This is a Buddhist type of meditation he engaged in when he got the idea of developing his mindfulness program. Vipassana is a word from the ancient Pali language of India, translated as "insight" or "clear awareness." This technique is based on the teachings of Buddha and was used to attain a deeper insight into ending suffering, referred to as Nirvana. According to Buddha's teachings, mindfulness is among the qualities developed during Vipassana meditation.

So far, we've established the connection between mindfulness and Buddhism, which influenced its latest revival. However, it is more evident in an ancient text Satipatthana Sutta, translated as The Discourse on the Establishing of Mindfulness (the word Sati means mindfulness) in English.

In Satipatthana Sutta, Buddha lays out mindfulness instructions that guide its practitioners to focus on the different aspects of experience. They are; the body, the mind, sensations, and mental contents.

It's important to note that Buddha's first foundation of mindfulness is the body. So it is not surprising to see modern mindfulness practices start by focusing on one or different aspects of the human experience.

Modern mindfulness is now taught with little or no mention of the Buddhist connection, even though a wealth of knowledge of this practice is rooted in Buddhism. Mindfulness is commonly described as a form of mental training, which is a helpful way to understand it. A great deal of research has gone into mindfulness and its benefits. In DBT, mindfulness skills are the core component of better emotion regulation.

THE ROLE OF MINDFULNESS IN DBT

Practicing mindfulness has been a life-changer for me. Even though the process sounds simple, it only works if practiced right.

A growing body of research suggests mindfulness-based interventions (MBIs) as an effective practice for decreasing stress, reducing rumination and emotional reactivity, and encouraging relationship satisfaction.

A study published in the National Library of Science, "Effects of Mindfulness on Psychological Health: A Review of Empirical Studies," showed the effects of mindfulness on psychological health by encouraging reduced psychological symptoms and emotional reactivity, increased subjective well-being, and improved behavioral regulation (Keng et al., 2011).

In another study, 20 novice mediators were tasked to participate in a 10-day intensive mindfulness meditation retreat. The group recorded less rumination, better memory capacity, sustained attention during a task and experienced few depressive symptoms after the retreat (Chambers et al., 2008).

In a newer study, researchers found that people who had been practicing mindfulness for many years could effectively disengage from emotionally upsetting pictures and focus better on the cognitive task than those who don't practice mindfulness (Ortner et al., 2007).

Another study suggests that mindfulness protects against the effect of emotionally stressful relationships by allowing you to express yourself better in social situations and give relationship satisfaction (Barnes et al., 2007).

In a meta-analysis of 39 studies showing the usefulness of MBSR, the researchers concluded that mindfulness is helpful in altering affective and cognitive processes that cause clinical issues (Hoffman et al., 2010).

During the day, many people spend only a tiny portion of their day mindfully engaged. They tend to zone out and get distracted by unhelpful thoughts. Instead of getting involved with reality, they prefer to get engaged with their thoughts and ideas, making it easy to lose sight of what is happening at that moment.

I was guilty of allowing my thoughts to consume me. As a result, I got distracted with tasks instead of staying mindful and enjoying the moment. However, being mindful means noticing your environment, expanding your attention, and enjoying the moment. Practicing this ancient skill is vital in DBT as it plays an essential role in helping people to be mindful, get better, and live the life of their dreams.

My time working as a sales representative in an organization was supposed to be enjoyable and fulfilling because it was one thing I've always wanted to do. I've always wanted to meet people, negotiate with them, and present and sell products or services to them. So, of course, I liked that aspect of the job. However, compiling the weekly and monthly reports was tedious and tiring; I was not too fond of that aspect of the job. Even though I only had to do this once a week and possibly, five times a month, it's still something I didn't look forward to doing. While compiling the reports, I was fond of making harsh judgments and saying difficult things to myself: "This is a total waste of time." "It's so boring and tiring!" "This is terrible." "I am tired of doing this." This continues, and instead of focusing on what I am doing and trying to get it right, my mind will keep wandering, telling me different kinds of unwanted stories about the task.

In hindsight, my actions triggered strong emotions such as resentment, anger, sadness, and despair. And it doesn't stop there! These emotions found a way to affect the rest of my day and even my week. As a result, I experienced a bad mood even when I was done with the task and made mistakes I considered silly because I should know better.

Instead of tolerating this tedious task, I allowed it to get to me and affect my mood. Whenever I am in a bad mood, I start having judgments, and what should be insignificant will cause me great suffering. As a result, I most likely will spend my day in a foul mood and feel worse, especially when I need to carry out my other responsibilities.

This is where mindfulness comes in. If I had been mindful of the dilemma above, I would've done better with the "supposed" unenjoyable task of curating my report. By practicing mindfulness, I should've approached the task with a spirit of acceptance and engaged in it without judgment. Whenever I notice any judgment, I should've turned my mind back to what I was doing, been aware of the sensations I felt holding a pen, and noticed the movements of my hands. By giving more attention to my environment, fully engaging in the task, and repeatedly turning my mind to it, I will provide little or no opportunity for negative attributions. This is how mindfulness can avert strong and unpleasant emotions.

Mindfulness allows you to train your brain and focus on what your senses tell you, calming your mind and body. It teaches you to consider your opinions, validate yourself, help you make better decisions, and avert emotional suffering. Instead of trying to suppress or quash certain emotions, mindfulness encourages permitting yourself to feel them.

When you're mindful, you'll observe what comes with emotions. The emotions will naturally go away the way they came if you don't give them too much attention. For example, you will notice your flushed face, lump in your throat, sweaty palms, and all other experiences without the intention of suppressing them. Since "you can’t argue with your emotions," the best approach is to tolerate them without holding or pushing them away.

We've discussed the main reasons mindfulness is used so much in DBT. When you recognize the power of mindfulness, even with a thousand distractions, you will notice them all and shift your attention to where it should be. It's more like fly fishing, where your mind will cast its line too far places if distracted, and then you can gently reel it back when you bring your mind to the present. The process will reoccur as much as needed. It will happen plenty of times in a short duration, and the more you practice, the easier it becomes to know when your mind has wandered. With each practice, you will gain more control and clarity.

THE 7 PRINCIPLES OF MINDFULNESS

Mindfulness encourages you to be more involved in the present moment and be aware of your breath, where you are, and what you're doing.

According to Kabat-Zinn, seven factors constitute the central pillars of mindfulness. Together, these factors can help you cultivate more awareness of the present moment, focus more on important things, and help you calm your anxious mind.

- **Non-judging**

Have you ever sat in a meeting, a classroom, or with someone talking to you and suddenly noticed that you've not been paying attention? If yes, this suggests that your mind has been busy and consumed with thoughts, drifting away from the moment. However, with your non-judging part, you will know when this happens and not be hard on yourself. It's like being an "impartial witness" to your experience by being aware of your experiences and letting the judgments go!

- **Patience**

When you try to incorporate what you've learned – sharpening focus, encouraging awareness and meditating, and you don't seem to get the hang of it, you'll feel frustrated, right? That's where the famous saying "Patience is a virtue" comes in." Don't expect immediate results; remember that mindfulness requires patience and taking small, consistent steps to see results. Understand that you need time and space for mindful practices, and things will happen in their own time.

- **Beginner's mind**

You'll easily lose yourself when you believe everything you hear, see, and experience. You need to be more open to the fact that no moment is the same as another, and with new things comes change. Have a clear, open, and uncluttered mind. Don't allow your experiences, expectations, and beliefs to keep you from seeing things in the present moment. Have a curious mind like that of a child.

- **Trust**

Having trust in yourself and your feelings is an important aspect of mindfulness. Trust your intuition, even if you make mistakes with them. It's better to look inwardly than outwardly for directions. The idea is to find wisdom from within and trust in the unfolding.

- **Non-striving**

Do you find yourself rushing and all charged up to achieve your goals? How often do you strive for the next big thing? If you are used to rushing everything, you need to slow down and focus on where you are. Mindfulness encourages focusing on seeing and accepting things as they are by embracing the moment you are in. Try not to overreact; hold onto your awareness.

- **Acceptance**

What you're doing here is protecting your energy. Many of the battles you're facing result from not letting things be as they are. When you acknowledge and accept such things, you can easily go with the flow without resistance or pushing against things. Although, acceptance can sometimes be misconstrued. Acceptance isn't being content with things you don't like; it's learning to accept things just how they are without being clouded by biases.

- **Letting go**

Is letting go that simple? Of course, letting go and relaxing can be difficult when you're fixated on your ideas and thoughts. However, not letting go will allow you to focus on things that don't matter, alleviating your worries and stress. By letting things go or being as they are, you get freed up from negative energy and do the things that bring you joy and happiness.

As you can see, the seven principles of mindfulness aim to help you find peace within yourself. Following them will keep you more balanced for a healthy and happy life.

There are many ways to incorporate practicing mindfulness into your daily life. This chapter has only covered the basics of mindfulness. The following chapter will discuss different mindful exercises you can start engaging in today!

3

MINDFULNESS TECHNIQUES TO HELP YOU LIVE IN THE PRESENT

Everything happens so fast! One moment, you're struggling to get your sleepy head up from bed, and after a few hours, it's nighttime, and you have to rest in anticipation of the next day's activities.

Rinse and repeat!

Sadly, this is how many people live their lives. They get carried away with what is to come that they forget to enjoy what they have now.

Each day comes with struggles and joys that we fail to recognize. We rush through our everyday activities, never stopping to enjoy the moment. This rush is probably part of what makes us anxious and worried.

During a challenging phase of my life, I found myself just breezing in and out of each day. It then began to accumulate over months. I had goals, but I couldn't achieve them. I woke up every morning feeling grumpy, ate my lousy breakfast, and went to work. At my workplace, I would continuously have disagreements with coworkers and then come home after work feeling angry. Finally, I would go to bed very tired and continue the cycle the next day. I was living my life with nothing to look forward to. My goals were left unattended, and my health suffered from my lack of mindfulness.

Living in the moment is difficult, especially when we have so much going on. Bills to pay, work to do, friends to spend time with, and a family that looks up to you. It's a lot!

People love to emphasize the value of being present in the moment and the various ways that doing so will help us. All of that sounds good, especially the reduced levels of tension and anxiety, but how can we live in the present if our minds are continually fixed on the past and worried about the future?

It is challenging to enjoy the now when regrets about the past or fear about the future consume our thoughts. Thankfully, I got out of that horrible feeling, and I am sure you can do it too.

Many basic techniques of mindfulness are helpful for people who struggle to live in the present. You can do little things every day to help you get over feelings of anxiety.

As I mentioned earlier, I had to figure out everything by myself, so it was hard initially. I used to believe practicing mindfulness meant sitting still with my knees crossed, my teeth clenched, and my hands folded. I used to sit on my balcony every night before going to sleep and do nothing! Although it was boring, I thought that was how I was supposed to feel. One night, I even dozed off on my balcony. The following morning, my body ached, and I was still irritable all day.

After a month of sitting, nothing changed, so I realized I was doing something wrong. So I did more research and finally found the answers I sought. As soon as I discovered that I could practice mindfulness in different and exciting ways, engaging became much easier.

Paying attention to the food while eating is a simple way to practice mindfulness. Focus solely on the food's warmth, crunchiness, and flavor rather than your phone or television. You can also practice mindfulness by taking note of the sound of the sand and you as you walk on it. If you've once tried to pay attention to your body, feelings, and surroundings, then you've practiced mindfulness.

But Why Mindfulness?

It's important to understand that mindfulness is not a fleeting mental state that appears during meditation and disappears for the rest of the day. Instead, mindfulness is a way of life that allows you to take a step back and be in the present in any situation you find yourself in.

Living in the present means letting go of worries about what has already happened and what might happen in the future. It means appreciating the present and living for the day.

Being mindful means being fully present and involved with whatever you are doing at the time, free from distractions, and conscious of your thoughts without becoming sucked into them.

Through meditation, you can develop the skill of mindfulness and practice it daily. By training your mind to be present, you also prepare yourself to live more mindfully – in the moment, breathing and feeling everything.

Mindfulness is an excellent way to reduce stress and increase focus, empathy, patience, energy, and happiness. Although mindfulness doesn't make stress or other problems disappear, it gives us more control over how we respond to them in the present. This increases our chances of responding in a composed and sympathetic manner when faced with stress or other issues. It also makes us deliberate about how we want to react.

HOW TO PRACTICE MINDFULNESS FOR SPECIFIC REASONS

There are countless possibilities every day! Start things off with a happy heart. Every morning, you have control over your attitude; keep it positive and hopeful. Enjoy every moment of the day to the fullest. Embrace as much of today as possible, including all the sights, sounds, scents, joys, and sorrows. These are all around you, but you overlook them or fail to appreciate them fully.

You can practice living in the moment by developing a mindfulness cue, learning to meditate, and engaging in random acts of kindness.

Mindfulness for mood swings

Mood swings are emotions that change quickly and firmly. We all feel agitated and cranky because our emotions can get irregular sometimes. We experience mood swings and lack energy whenever this happens. While mood swings might occasionally be natural, they can also indicate a more serious problem like depression or anxiety.

Fortunately, research has shown that practicing mindfulness helps you control your mood swings, slows down your thoughts, and improves your ability to manage emotional ups and downs by becoming more aware of how your mind works.

Have you ever given it a shot? You should try it!

- Close your eyes, relax, and breathe in and out slowly.
- Try to find your breath slowly. Where can you feel it the most?
- Focus on the breath as though you were just noticing it for the first time. For example, you can focus on your abdomen or the tip of your nose as you breathe.
- Simply notice the air entering your lungs, and as you exhale, notice the air coming out.
- Your thoughts will try to stray, so you should be conscious of this. Gently refocus your attention on where it is supposed to be.
- Say "straying" to yourself when your mind starts to wander. It will help bring your attention back to the breath so that you can just observe it.
- As your mind wanders, gently bring it back to the breath. Then, you can continue until you finally get over your mood swings.

Mindfulness for urges and impulses

Urges and impulses usually peak between 20 and 30 minutes. The temptation will pass if you are determined not to do anything about it. However, by giving in to your urges and impulses, you are making them stronger.

- Take time to think about a recent urge that you felt. Try to take note of every feeling that arises as you think about this urge. Then, pay attention to how these feelings change over time.

- Sit in a peaceful environment, close your eyes and focus only on the area of your body where you frequently experience these urges.
- Pay close attention to it. If more than one part of your body is connected to an urge, focus on the part where you feel the urge the most.
- Keep track of the feelings you are experiencing in this body part. How does it feel?
- For around two minutes, pay attention to your breathing.
- After that, bring your focus back to the area of your body where you are experiencing the urge. Observe whatever feelings arise in these areas.
- If observing the sensations becomes too difficult, gradually bring your focus back to your breathing for a short while before returning to the areas with the urge again.
- Keep doing these things until the impulse passes.

Mindfulness for anger

In addition to reducing stress, mindfulness improves your relationship with yourself and helps you control powerful emotions like anger. When you're angry, you tend to forget that you have the option to press pause and cool down. Instead, you want to do the worst in a fit of rage.

When you practice mindfulness in the heat of the moment, you have taught yourself how to deal with your anger rather than adding fuel to the fire. It's possible to respond from a calmer, more collected place, regardless of how agitated you feel. You simply have to connect with your emotions.

You may need to use these tips on mindfulness if you experience intense anger that negatively impacts your relationships or escalates into bigger fights.

- Place your hands comfortably at your sides, eyes slightly closed, and sit in a relaxed position.
- Take a few deep breaths to fill your torso with air, and then exhale fully.
- Think of a time when you got angry. Imagine what took place and allow yourself to feel the fury once again.
- When you think back to the incident, other feelings could come to mind, such as sadness.
- The urge to attempt to push it away can come to you. Instead, let the feeling of fury grow intense, though to a safe level. Examine these feelings.
- Allow your emotions to linger before slowly returning your focus to your breath. Take deep breaths.
- Think about your feelings. What feelings did you notice? Did the feelings change while you were observing them? Where did the anger go at the end? Did your anger become stronger or weaker as you became aware of it?

Mindfulness for self-compassion and self-esteem

There will always be someone more successful, wealthy, attractive, intelligent, or powerful than you are. It doesn't mean you should feel bad or be harsh to yourself. This brings us to self-compassion and self-esteem!

Self-esteem is the opinion you have about yourself. Self-compassion makes you feel good about yourself because it does not involve assessing how deserving you are. Instead, you get to give yourself the same compassion you offer others when they fail or feel inadequate.

Practicing mindfulness for self-compassion and esteem will help you make life more manageable and feel better about yourself.

- Sit in an upright position with your hands on your lap.
- Breathe slowly and steadily, taking note of your chest's gentle rise and fall. Do this for five minutes.
- Make yourself happy by imagining things you love, like a smile or the sea.
- Think about someone who makes you feel good and consider what makes you love them.
- Then silently say positive things to yourself out loud. "I am worthy of love. I am gorgeous. I accept myself as I am. I am concerned about my feelings and challenges." As you say these, put your hand over your heart and breathe deeply.

- If you notice that your thoughts are beginning to stray, return to your breath.
- Sit until you start feeling good about yourself.

Mindfulness for fear of abandonment

Going through numerous breakups was tough for me. At one point, I feared that no one would want me. When I eventually got into a relationship again, I was scared that the lady would leave me like the others.

Typically the fear of abandonment can come from a parent, sibling, friend, or lover. Suppose you are going through situations that are similar to mine. Then, this mindfulness exercise would be beneficial for you.

- Sit down and clear your mind of all thoughts. Make sure the area you choose to stay in is quiet and well-ventilated.
- Place your hands on your chest and breathe slowly. Inhale, hold your breath for a while and then let it go, slowly. Feel the air going in and coming out for about five minutes.
- Think of someone you love so dearly. Let the feeling of love radiate and envelope you.
- While holding your hand on your chest, say things like, "I release all fear to make room for love. The things that leave me aren't meant for me. The things that are meant for me stay with me. I only

lose that which I claim to. I release darkness to let light in."

- Always take a breath in after each affirmation. Then, continue this exercise until you feel yourself let go of any negative emotions.

Mindfulness for emptiness

Do you feel incomplete or empty sometimes? This exercise will help you cool off and believe in yourself.

- Sit comfortably and place your hands on your lap.
- Start taking deep breaths, slowly and steadily.
- Think of a part of your body where you feel incomplete or empty. Place your hands on it and breathe.
- Inhale through your nose and exhale through your mouth.
- Make sure you're deep breathing. Be sure that the breath fills your whole body, from your head to the tip of your toes. Then, exhale.
- Do this for at least 25 minutes or until you feel you've had enough

MINDFUL BREATHING

Isn't it amazing that something as small as breathing can hold so much power? Breaths can calm your worries and help you feel better about yourself. The best thing is that you can do these breathing exercises anytime to calm down your emotions.

There are five ways to practice breathing, each with its peculiarities.

- **Mindful breathing**: This exercise focuses on the breath's regular occurrence; it does not include breath manipulation. Focusing on a physical cue, such as the rise and fall of your stomach and the feeling of the breath in your nose, can be helpful. The first step is to start breathing normally while paying close attention to your breath.
- **Counting breaths**: This method of breathing uses another mental cue to keep us focused: counting each breath. You'll find it challenging to keep track of your breath; counting is a way for you to remain focused. Those with highly active thoughts should practice this breathing.
- **Deep inhalation**: To achieve the intended result in this situation, you must deepen your breath. Deep breathing, commonly called belly breathing or diaphragmatic breathing, helps ease anxiety and foster serenity. It helps to deactivate the stress response by inhaling deeply into the belly and exhaling fully.
- **2-4 breathing**: This kind of breath entails lengthening the exhalation such that it exceeds the

inhalation. For example, take a two-count inhale and a four-count exhale.

- **Energizing breaths**: You can use your breath to energize yourself if you're feeling lazy. Fill the lungs with air in four equal yet distinct breaths, then let it all out in one long, smooth exhale.

MINDFUL WALKING

Walking mindfully means paying attention to our breath and each step we take as we walk. You can do it wherever you are, whether you're by yourself enjoying nature, in the parking lot, or in your neighborhood. However, it's best to be in nature as it increases the calming effect, ultimately slowing down your brain waves.

The mind becomes distracted when it is left alone. Trying mindful walking helps us gather awareness and be conscious of the environment.

- Walk at a comfortable pace. Place your hands wherever it is most comfortable for you.
- Count up to ten steps and then start over from one again.
- Pay attention to how your foot rises and falls as you walk. Also, take note of how your legs and other parts of your body move. Keep an eye out for any side-to-side movement of your body.

- Your mind will stray, so gently bring it back as much as you need to without getting frustrated.
- Expand your focus on sounds during the next five minutes. Recognize sounds for what they are: sounds. The blaring horns, the chirping birds, notice everything.
- Pay attention to your sense of smell: the wet grass, the smell of wall paint. Pay attention to whatever it tells you without forcing yourself to feel anything.
- Move on to the vision, including the colors, objects, and everything else you see.
- No matter where you are, be mindful of everything around you. Nothing has to be changed, fixed, or done.
- Now, observe your feet touching the ground, and be aware of how it feels. Then stand still for a moment and breathe slowly. Do this until you feel yourself become calm.

MINDFUL EATING

With mindful eating, we can fully enjoy our food at the moment without worrying about our diet or any of the other rules that go along with it.

When we practice mindful eating, we pay attention to our senses and how the food makes us feel.

The goal is not to lose weight. Instead, the goal is to inspire people to enjoy the eating experience fully and to help them relish the present and the meal. This will, in turn, allow them to eat cautiously.

- Sit down and hold a raisin in your hand. Look at the raisin as if it were the first time.
- Be mindful of the raisin's form, texture, color, and size as you observe it. Is it hard or soft?
- Smell the raisin. Don't you just want to throw it in your mouth already? Is it hard to resist the urge to eat it immediately?
- How tiny does the raisin feel in your hand? Take a bite of the raisin and pay attention to what your tongue is saying.
- Bite into the raisin very cautiously. Chew thrice, then stop.
- Describe the raisin's flavor. Which texture is it? What does it taste like? How does it feel on your tongue?
- Swallow it. How does it make you feel?

The raisin experience is a beautiful illustration of what mindful eating is. It lets us concentrate on the experience. In order to practice mindful eating, we need to have these seven attitudes.

- **Non-Judging:** Your preconceived notions about raisins are the first thing you encounter in this experience. Do you approve of them?
- **Patience:** Mindful eating requires patience, and being present moment by moment demands consistent practice.
- **Beginner's mentality:** By approaching your experiences in the same way that a newborn does (taking one taste, one glance, one touch, one smell, one sound), you can be receptive to whatever their current meaning is.
- **Trust:** We get more tolerant of ourselves and thus more trustworthy by being aware of and enjoying how we feel and how different foods affect us.
- **Non-Striving:** This is obviously in contrast to dieting. Dieting means that we entirely focus on attempting to lose weight. In mindful eating, you, as an eater, are free to be present and truly appreciate the experience because you aren't expecting any particular outcome.
- **Acceptance:** Mindfulness is a practice that involves learning to be willing to observe what occurs and accepting it. It might be accepting the good (the delicious flavor of only one raisin) or the bad (our dislike of raisins). Accept whatever arises in the moment. What is, is what is.
- **Letting go:** To eat mindfully, we must let go of our past experiences with food. When we let go, we can

expect new things in the present moment without judging the food by our former beliefs.

BODY SCANS

Our muscles can be relaxed thanks to mindful body scans, which help us reconnect with our bodies and find peace. The scan is divided into three parts: the head, the upper body, and the lower body.

- Sit comfortably and relax.
- For five minutes, observe how your feet interact with the ground.
- Keep an eye on how they make touch with the ground underneath you. Also, observe how your feet are feeling.
- Do your feet need rest? Lift your focus to the lowest portions of your legs, just above your feet. Be conscious of any feelings you may have there.
- Bring your focus gradually to your knees. Observe how your knee makes contact with the chair you are sitting on.
- Pay attention to your buttocks region now. Pay attention to how your body interacts with the chair.
- Your upper body comes next. Feel your abdomen. Is it relaxed, or is it tense? Pay attention to every feeling, no matter how slight. Focus on your lower

back now. Observe how it makes contact with the chair's back.

- Now, bring your attention to your hands. Be mindful of any feelings you may experience. Are your hands lying in your lap or on the chair? Feel how your hands and lap connect.
- Move to your head. Pay close attention to your neck and shoulder muscles. Pay attention to how that area is feeling. Do you feel any muscle tension?
- Shift your focus to the top of your head. Pay attention to your lips, nose, eyes, and then ears. Do you have any physical aches or tension? Pay attention to how your head feels. If your thoughts begin to stray, gently bring them back.

And that's it for mindfulness! The next chapter will discuss how to handle intense moments when you encounter a crisis.

4

WHAT IS DISTRESS TOLERANCE?

You'll likely experience extreme emotional states and crises at some point in life. Sometimes, the crises may be as big as a layoff from your dream job, a divorce, or even the death of a loved one. Other times, the crises may be as minor as missing the bus, a long line at your favorite coffee shop, or heavy traffic during rush hour; those times, you don't know what to wear to a date or when you can't find your keys. Distress tolerance skills can get you to a more manageable place where you can survive crises.

I can still remember a few years ago when my roommate and I heatedly argued over the type of Christmas lights and decorations to get for our minuscule Christmas tree housing in our shared apartment. My friend had simply laughed at a comment I had made. However, what started as a decision over candy canes or globe lights escalated quickly. I couldn't explain why I felt so angry, chest-heaving anger that eventually led to an outburst from me. Sadly, I shouted a rain of not-so-nice words at him, bringing up a few things he had shared with me in confidence.

The situation got so bad he didn't spend Christmas at our apartment that year and eventually moved out a few months later. One of the many failed relationships left me with questions and doubts about myself. I didn't know what came over me, it felt somewhat satisfactory only at that moment, and I couldn't stop myself till I had run out of what to say.

You may have experienced this kind of uncontrollable outbursts, impulses to act irrationally, or felt overwhelming fear when dealing with an emotional crisis. You are not alone in this, and there are scientifically proven ways to deal with the surge of emotions in such moments to achieve safer and better outcomes.

Distress tolerance is a vital DBT skill that can help you make mindful decisions, save you from facing more stress and anxiety and understand what is going on in your own mind.

This chapter discusses how something as simple as deep breaths and counting numbers frees you from the control of your emotions and redirects your mind to work for you rather than against you. It was not until I understood and applied these methods that the happy and fulfilling life I wanted started to look less like a dream and more like reality.

WHAT IS DISTRESS TOLERANCE?

Distress tolerance is the ability to tolerate and survive an emotional crisis without worsening it. It involves a set of skills that helps people handle actual or perceived distress. We all experience a wide range of stress in our lives, from small daily worries such as an annoying boss, an impatient child, or falling out with a friend to significant experiences like the death of a loved one, a business going bankrupt, or a divorce. For some people, a response to stress includes negative emotions that can be overwhelming and unbearable.

When someone has a low distress tolerance, little too mildly stressful situations that translate into emotional stress can overwhelm someone, resulting in potential negative responses or reactions such as self-harm or impulsive behavior. Therefore, learning and practicing distress tolerance skills can positively influence your ability to handle difficult emotions.

In some cases, reality acceptance is the best way to deal with the stress that plagues our thoughts. You can't exactly ignore your emotions but accepting that certain things are beyond your control helps to focus your energy on the things that are within your ability to do. You have to be willing to accept reality because you can't fight it, and to keep struggling leads to more suffering.

In other situations, discovering your triggers and understanding you can't make things better immediately helps you navigate and tolerate painful events, emotions, and impulses easier without making them worse.

In the past, traditional medicine and therapy were centered around stressful situation avoidance to become more stable and equipped to handle stressful emotions, but how much control do you have over that? For some, this increases your misery by forcing you to actively consider what situations may or may not be a trigger. This is why DBT focuses on newer practices and therapies that recognize and accept stressful situations and teaches you to work around them properly. You can take these practices on your own or with the help of a professional.

Now that you know what distress tolerance is and how it affects your stress response let's discuss what goes on in the body when you feel stressed.

The Physiological Effects of Stress

When you feel stress, the body responds the same way it does to threats from predators, aggressors, and harm. This response is adaptive, i.e., changes to prepare the body to handle the threat presented by an internal or external emotional challenge by taking a protective path.

Living in a fast-paced world, we face many attention-demanding activities every day. These activities could be our daily workload, taking care of the family, running an errand, or anything requiring us to put in mental or physical energy.

Your body is designed and wired to react and protect itself from external and internal threats, including stress.

Over time, these activities will build up stress, and your body will view these changes as threats and react accordingly. As a result of the counter from your body, you may feel like you're under attack.

Whether it's worrying about relationships, your kids, a mortgage, pressure at work, meeting a deadline, or persistently being under psychological pressure can stimulate your body into triggering a rush of stress hormones that produce physiological changes. For example, stress can fasten your breath and make your heart pound rapidly, sometimes causing beads of sweat, dizziness, and tense muscle.

These intuitive feelings can make life miserable – but you can fight back! You don't have to live in perpetual fear by allowing stress to control your life.

Automatic stress response

When your body feels threatened, for example, hearing a sudden loud sound while you are totally relaxed and unprepared will set off the danger alarm in a small region in your brain called the hypothalamus, alerting your entire system. At the same time, your hormonal and nerve signals will prompt the adrenal glands at the top of the kidney to release a surge of hormones such as cortisol and adrenaline, boosting your energy in return.

It is a complex natural alarm system that communicates with the brain to control motivation, fear, and mood. While adrenaline elevates your blood pressure, increases your heart rate, and improves energy supply, cortisol, on the other hand, increases glucose in the bloodstream, improves the availability of substance-repairing tissues, and enhances the use of glucose in the brain. In addition, cortisol controls harmful or unimportant functions of the fight-or-flight situation, suppresses the digestive system, growth process, and reproductive system, and changes the immune system.

When the natural stress response goes wild

Your body's stress response system can be self-limiting because your hormones will return to normal when a perceived threat passes. For example, when the cortisol and adrenaline levels drop, your blood pressure and heart rate will return to baseline, with other systems resuming their regular routines. However, the fight-or-flight response will stay on stressors and will constantly be present, and you will feel like you are under attack.

Overexposure to cortisol and stress hormones and long-term activation of your stress response can interrupt all your body processes, putting you at risk of health conditions such as:

- Headaches
- Anxiety
- Depression

- Digestive issues
- Weight gain
- Insomnia
- Muscle tension and pain
- Memory and concentration impairment
- Heart attack, heart disease, high blood pressure, and stroke

Due to the risk of having these issues above, you need to learn healthy ways of coping with life stressors.

WHAT DOES THE VAGUS NERVE HAVE TO DO WITH THIS?

The vagus nerve is the longest cranial nerve in the body. It starts behind your ears, runs through your body, and then to the gut. 75% of parasympathetic nerve fibers originate from the vagus nerve. So your sympathetic nervous system will kick in when there's a perceived real or fake threat. The parasympathetic nervous system is tasked with calming your body down.

The function of the vagus nerve is to make you calm when you feel stressed and to alert you when you're no longer in danger. It's like helping you to "rest and digest." This action is a low-tone dorsal activity. On the other hand, the parasympathetic is a high tone activity when you're in freeze mode.

If you aren't emotionally healthy, you are either sympathetic (the fight or flight mode) or parasympathetic (the freeze mode). These aren't the only states of parasympathetic. The two other states are the rest and digest and the ventral vagal branch of the parasympathetic for social engagement (Polyvagal Theory). The function of the ventral vagal is to make you feel less guarded.

According to psychiatrists, the vagal tone can regulate stress responses through meditation and yoga, especially the breathing techniques it encourages. You can resume self-regulating vagal function using mindfulness, breath work, and grounding techniques. This activity will likely improve resilience, mood, and anxiety symptoms.

Vagus Nerve Stimulation (VNS) is a treatment that involves a device looking like a "peacemaker-like" device. When the device is implanted and the vagus nerve is stimulated, you are tapping into being in the present moment and coming home to yourself.

When you're in a difficult situation, you're lighting your vagus nerve and turning inwardly to check in with your true feelings. At that moment that you sing, shout, or speak, you're igniting your vagus nerve. This is why some of these emotions can be emotional for many people.

DISTRESS TOLERANCE AND VAGUS NERVE STIMULATION (VNS)

Distress tolerance is preparing for a stressful event before it happens. Sometimes, you may be unable to overcome the initial shock you feel or the fight or flight response. As a result, the brain can't put coping strategies into place. So, VNS is responsible for restoring the sympathetic system.

When you're experiencing high stress, your body will stay in high gear while stress hormones such as cortisol and adrenaline flow through the body. As a result, the action will create wear and tear on the body and mind, resulting in health problems over time.

Luckily, your body has its own superpower that decreases the fight or flight response. The VNS is responsible for counterbalancing the fight or flight system, triggering a relaxation response.

The vagus nerve is a significant part of how your body and brain function. Without this cranial nerve, your body can't do basic activities. Stimulating it gives many benefits. Some of the ways you can stimulate your vagus nerve include:

- **Breathing techniques**

With breathing exercises such as deep and slow belly breathing, you can shift your focus from the pain or stress you're experiencing. Your mind processes one thing at a time, so when you're focused on the rhythm of your breath, you won't be focused on the stressor or pain.

You can practice deep breathing by inhaling through your nose and exhaling through your mouth. Remember to breathe slowly and deeply from your belly and exhale longer than you inhale to trigger the relaxation response.

- **Cold water immersion**

This involves immersing your forehead (close your eyes) and your cheeks in cold water for a few seconds. This will trigger the vagus nerve, activate the immune system, and decrease heart rate.

- **Laughter**

Who would've thought that having a good laugh can stimulate your vagus nerve, improve your mood, and boost your immune system? In fact, if I were you, I'd make good use of this activity which has zero cost.

- **Massage**

A gentle or firm touch on your body can stimulate the vagus nerve. You can do it yourself or use a professional for this. You can massage your body by applying two pumps of massage oil to your hands, cupping your hands to your nose, and inhaling it. Then you start massaging your neck, starting from the clavicle. Next, move to your ears by rubbing your earlobes, chest, and all over your body until you experience a sensation of a yawn or sigh.

A massage can give you a soothing feeling and bring you to a relaxed state when you feel stressed.

You can make the best out of the techniques for stimulating the vagus nerve by keeping a record or journal of how the techniques make you feel in different situations. This should help you know the right one to implement in a given situation. Write down if one was more effective than the other.

Once you can control the immediate surge of emotions, you will be able to implement some of the distress tolerance techniques we will cover in the next chapter.

5

PUTTING DISTRESS TOLERANCE INTO PRACTICE

As I've explained, distress tolerance is the ability to manage emotional situations without feeling overwhelmed. Be it perceived or real; emotional stress can be challenging to manage, especially for individuals with a trauma history. This inability to cope with distress may worsen during a crisis, leaving you helpless and out of control.

Since there is a way out of those times when you feel hated, unloved, and unlucky, we'll be focusing on putting distress tolerance skills into practice. Distress tolerance skills help you learn how to survive a crisis. This chapter will teach you how to handle difficult emotions and learn how to quickly return to a calm state when you encounter stressors.

Imagine this scenario...

You have a big presentation at work tomorrow. You're excited because this could set you up for a significant promotion if you execute it right. But you're also nervous. "What if I mess it up?" "What if it doesn't go the way that I anticipated?"

Your nerves are all frazzled due to excitement and nervousness. To calm yourself down, you decide to hang out with friends and have a few drinks, nothing harmful. You've found that spending time with your closest friends when a major event arises always helps with the nerves. So, you go out with them.

The next day, you wake up half an hour before the presentation. Alarmed, you jump out of bed and fumble through your morning routine. Quickly, you rush to call a taxi and make it just in time for the presentation. "Whew, that was close," you say as you prepare to do the presentation.

Now, imagine this second scenario...

Instead of going out with friends the night before your big presentation, you decide to prepare. So, you get your outfit ready and place it where you can quickly find it and put it on the next day. You also set your alarm to wake you up an hour and thirty minutes before the go-time.

The next day, you wake up and go through your morning routine as usual without rushing or fumbling. You even make it to the office in time to have a coffee and review your presentation once more before going to the conference room to nail it.

Which of these two scenarios seems like the best? The answer is pretty apparent to anyone reading, but one thing I've observed is that crisis management isn't always as easy in practice. Well, unless you hone your skills!

It's one thing to be familiar with DBT distress tolerance skills and another to know how to incorporate them into your daily life. Still, without knowledge of practical techniques, it's not always easy to put distress tolerance into practice. Fortunately, that's exactly what I'll be explaining in this chapter. I should tell you that while the application may take a while to learn, it's always worth it.

This chapter aims to help you learn practical skills for managing disruptive behavior. I'll discuss seven skills, so let's get to it.

TIPP

You're at your breaking point emotionally. Maybe a situation has spiraled entirely out of your control, or this just happened to be the "last straw." In this situation, I recommend the distress tolerance skill called TIPP. TIPP is an acronym for Temperature, Intense Exercise, Paced Breathing, and Paired Muscle Relaxation. It's precisely what you need.

The TIPP skills alter your body chemistry to bring you off the metaphorical ledge. In other words, they reduce your overwhelming feelings in a crisis. I like TIPP because it quickly defuses your emotions and reduces the intensity to a reasonable degree. Usually, I feel a reduction in emotional arousal within a few seconds or minutes of practicing it.

You'll love these skills because they're relatively easy to practice and don't require a lot of thinking or waiting. Another reason is that you can practice them anywhere, even in public. They are easily accessible without the side effects or cost of medication.

With dedicated practice, you can make TIPP skills an adaptive coping technique that you can use anywhere at any time.

- **T - Temperature**

Ever watched a Hollywood movie where the character suddenly scrambled out of a room to the restroom where they splashed a handful of water on their face? Most likely! You probably don't realize it, but that's a TIPP skill in use.

When you're emotionally aroused, your body might feel hot and feverish. You can change your temperature by splashing cold water on your face, signaling your brain to slow everything down. The brain will then activate the "mammalian dive reflex," which triggers a calming physiological response, such as reduced heart rate. Another way to achieve this is to take a 1 minute cold shower or hold some ice in your hands.

Changing your temperature prevents you from remaining in a heightened emotional state.

- **I - Intense Exercise**

Like temperature, intense exercise changes your body chemistry adaptively. It releases the stress you're feeling in the moment. This means performing an intense activity that matches the intensity of your emotion.

Intense exercise works because it's impossible to feel distressed and emotionally excited simultaneously. During that exercise, your heart rate increases, and your adrenaline pumps faster than ever. When your brain floods the body with adrenaline, you feel euphoria.

I recommend doing aerobic exercise for 15 to 20 minutes. It helps with releasing pent-up anger or frustration; it's also great to brighten your mood and pump yourself with energy. I have observed that even a few jumping jacks in one spot help with this if I am unable to do a 20-minutes exercise.

- **P - Paced Breathing**

Paced breathing is when you control your breath by exhaling slower and longer than when you inhale. Even something as simple as this can help manage emotional arousal. Breathing exercises are numerous, and anyone will work just fine. If you already have a breathing routine, stick to your usual routine. Otherwise, you can practice the "box breathing" technique, which I find pretty effective.

With paced breathing, each breath interval should be four seconds long. Inhale deeply for four seconds, hold your breath for four seconds, exhale for four seconds, and hold for four seconds before taking in the air again. Continue to use this breathing technique until you feel your body become calm. Consistent breathing deactivates your fight or flight response, relieving your body of tension.

- **P - Paired Muscle Relaxation**

The science behind this technique fascinates me. I tighten a voluntary muscle group, relax it, and allow it to rest - making the muscle more relaxed than before tightening. Relaxed muscles don't use as much oxygen as tensed ones, so breathing and heart rate automatically slow down. When this happens, it's impossible to remain emotionally agitated!

Try the PMR technique on a group of muscles, like the ones in your arms. Or work from toe to head or head to toe - you decide. Tighten the muscle as hard as you can in four seconds. Then, release the tension. Wait for each muscle group to relax before moving on to the next. By the end of the rounds, your entire body should feel fully relaxed.

The TIPP skills will bring you closer to productively coping with your emotions and making constructive decisions during a crisis.

ACCEPTS

The ACCEPTS distress tolerance technique combines skills to cope with a negative emotion until you're ready to deal with it or resolve the situation that triggered the emotion.

Let's say you're at work and you receive a text saying, "We need to have a conversation later today" from your girlfriend. You'll most likely wonder if it's a good or bad conversation you're about to have. That can put you in psychological distress as you wait for the day to end.

Eventually, when you're ready, you'll use skills such as interpersonal effectiveness to meet your needs. In this scenario, the distress tolerance skill you need is ACCEPTS: Activities, Contributing, Comparisons, Emotions, Push Away, Thoughts, and Sensation. These skills will help you to cope with distress until you can appropriately resolve the situation.

- **A - Activities**

Engage in a healthy activity. Take a walk, read a book, watch a movie, do the dishes, bake snacks, call a close friend, immerse yourself in work - just do anything that can keep you busy and take your mind off the upcoming conversation.

Move to another activity if you finish early. You may end up having a very productive day while awaiting the dreaded conversation.

- **C - Contributing**

Providing service to others can relieve distress in more than one way. Contributing distracts you from your distress by keeping your mind focused on someone or something else.

An act of service is any activity that makes you feel good about yourself while keeping your mind off the situation at hand. So, volunteer to babysit your friend's daughter while she's out, help your friend shop for something, bake cookies for a neighbor, or mow your relative's lawn. Simply go out and be of service to someone.

- **C - Comparisons**

Compare the "you" of today to the "you" of five years ago - it helps. The goal here is to put your present into perspective. Remind yourself of a time when you coped with challenges much harder than you do today. You aren't trying to invalidate your distress; you're reminding yourself that you've been in worse situations in the past.

If that doesn't work, compare yourself to someone who's experienced more pain or suffering than you. This skill helps you to gain a different perspective on your current situation.

- **E - Emotions**

Distract yourself from negative emotions by cultivating positive ones. Listen to upbeat music, read an inspirational book, or watch a happy sitcom. By doing this you can evoke the opposite of the distressed feeling you're experiencing.

It would be best if you did something with the opposite emotion for this technique to work. If you're anxious, watch a comedy. If you're angry, watch a romantic movie. Doing so changes your emotion and puts you in a different place.

- **P - Pushing Away**

Leave a distressing situation mentally by pushing it away from your mind temporarily. When you can't deal with an emotion or situation just yet, it's okay to push it away. I find this skill useful when I don't have a solution immediately. The goal isn't avoidance but to find respite, no matter how short.

Every time the situation sneaks up on your mind, block it out mentally. Use this technique to take a break from the pain. Or replace it with another thought, preferably a soothing one. You haven't found a solution to the problem, but you've put it away so that you can focus on more pleasant events in your life for the moment.

- **T - Thoughts**

Replace distressing thoughts with busy ones, such as counting from 100 to 1 or reciting the alphabet backward in your mind. You can even try solving a sudoku puzzle. These distracting thoughts keep your mind busy, preventing you from turning to self-destructive behavior until you achieve emotional regulation.

- **S - Sensation**

This final ACCEPTS skill involves using a strong stimulus (physical) to detach from the feelings of distress and, therefore, distract yourself from the pain. You'll find this particularly helpful if your distress triggers self-destructive or self-harming behavior.

Anything that triggers either of your five senses can help you cope with the pain. You could take a warm bath, put ice on your body, try eating your comfort snack, or watch your favorite show.

IMPROVE

Intense emotions are temporary. Whether it's a big or small circumstance, there will be many instances where you can't control a distressing event. In such situations, you'll need a distress tolerance skill to help you survive the crisis without resorting to unhealthy coping behaviors. The IMPROVE skill can help you learn to tolerate intense emotions until they subside.

IMPROVE is an acronym for Imagery, Meaning, Prayer, Relaxation, One thing in the moment, Vacation, and Encouragement.

- **I - Imagery:** Visualize yourself handling the problem successfully. Imagine the feeling of accomplishment when you're done. In doing so, you may even turn the tide in your favor by changing the outcome.
- **M - Meaning:** Find meaning in a painful situation. What lesson is there for you? Maybe you'll learn to build stronger bonds. Perhaps you'll become more empathetic. Maybe this will set you on the path to healing. Try to see the reason for your present situation.
- **P - Prayer:** You don't have to be religious to pray. Prayer is whatever works for you. If you believe in a higher power, you can pray to God or the Universe. Let go of your problems and ask the higher power to help you tolerate the pain a little longer.
- **R - Relaxation:** Stressful situations trigger the fight or flight response, which makes you tense up. Find activities to relax to relieve psychological distress. This could be anything from Yoga to deep breathing exercises to taking a relaxing walk in nature.
- **O - One thing in the moment:** Let go of the past and the future by grounding yourself in the moment.

Thinking of the past or worrying about the future will only compound the present suffering; it won't solve the problem. Find an activity you can devote yourself to in the moment.

- **V - Vacation:** An ideal vacation allows you to break free from your problems and stressors until you return home, ready to take on the world. But how many of us can take a vacation during a crisis? So, take a mental vacation instead. Visualize yourself lounging on a beach in Ibiza or driving along the Pacific Coast. Stay in that moment for as long as you need to de-stress.
- **E - Encouragement:** Internal encouragement can make a difference in distress tolerance. Encourage yourself with self-affirming phrases that mean something to you. "I got this!" "I am enough." "I can do this on my own!" Say it out loud.

You can use IMPROVE skills anywhere and anytime in a situation you can't control or change. Practice them consistently in minor situations, and they will manifest naturally in major ones.

STOP

STOP is a DBT distress tolerance skill used to ride out a crisis. The mnemonic is pretty easy to remember. Each letter stands for the following

- **S - Stop**

Freeze. Stop dead in your tracks. Don't move. Imagine that there's a red STOP sign right in front of you. Don't react to your emotions instantaneously. Don't let them control you in that heated moment when you're brimming with energy.

- **T - Take a step back**

Take a literal step back, or do it in your mind. Detach yourself from the intense urge to react to the emotion you're experiencing. Once you take that step back, pay attention to your breathing. It may be deep and shallow, or you may be holding it. Whatever it is, take a few deep breaths as slowly as possible.

- **O - Observe**

Observe everything happening within and around you. Pay attention to people in your environment; what are they saying or doing? Notice your thoughts and feelings. In a crisis, we tend to zoom in on a closed perspective instead of seeing the bigger picture. Unfortunately, that restricts us to a slice of information. You must see the whole picture to decide on the best course of action.

- **P - Proceed mindfully**

Use mindfulness techniques to ground yourself in the present moment before making a decision. Consult your wise mind to know what to do, and remind yourself that reacting impulsively won't give you a long-term solution.

Apply the STOP skill in the heat of the moment to ensure you don't do something you'll eventually regret.

RADICAL ACCEPTANCE

You'll often find yourself in undesirable situations that won't change. It's okay if you don't like or approve of the situation, but you must accept it to feel at peace. Before I learned about DBT, I used to try everything possible to change something I didn't like. It took a while before I realized that I couldn't change some things - all I could do was accept and make peace with them.

Radical acceptance is the acknowledgment that you have choices; sometimes, you have to choose whether or not you're willing to accept the reality of a situation. Accept and move forward with your life or choose to stay miserable.

Imagine you're laid off at work. You can't believe it. You try to deny it. So, you continue to do some tasks and forward them to your supervisor. But deep down, you know you've been fired. To avoid the pain, you bury yourself in work you shouldn't be doing.

This feels like it's working out just fine, except that time could have been invested in finding a new job. Instead, you find that you have so many unpaid bills, most of your savings are gone, and you are still unemployed.

With radical acceptance, you can accept that you're afraid you won't get a new job. Getting kicked into the unemployed market will make you miserable, but you need to start working on finding a new job, or forging your own path. Or else, you'll find yourself financially desolate.

So, you fire up your laptop and start applying to jobs you're qualified for or finding new ways to make money. Choosing to focus on the present instead of what may or may not happen will feel genuinely liberating.

Here are ten steps to radical acceptance:

1. Acknowledge that you're fighting or refusing reality.
2. Remind yourself that you cannot change reality, no matter how unpleasant it is.
3. Accept that there are reasons for this new reality. "This is how this happened."
4. Practice accepting reality with your body, mind, and spirit. Use mindfulness, self-talk, imagery, and relaxation techniques to practice acceptance.
5. Write out the things you would do if you could accept the facts as they are. Then, do these things as if you've already accepted.

6. Imagine accepting the unacceptable and practicing in your mind what the next step would be if you did.
7. Notice your body sensations as you imagine that.
8. Allow yourself to feel the associated emotion, grief, disappointment, or sadness. Let it wash over you.
9. Accept that you can still live a worthwhile life even in pain.
10. Try the pros and cons if you're still resisting acceptance.

SELF-SOOTHE

When in a heightened state of stress or anxiety, it becomes challenging to draw upon your natural self-soothing ability. When your levels of distress increase, it helps to have a readily accessible self-care toolkit. That way, you can manage the present moment more skillfully.

Self-soothing skills allow you to calm down and center yourself in times of distress to return to a more grounded place. You can self-soothe effectively during a crisis by utilizing emotional regulation skills and mindfulness with your senses.

- **Sight**

Try sitting outside your porch and gaze upon nature attentively with mindful eyes. Walk to the nearest park or take a leisurely hike up the hills. Sit outdoors at nighttime and feed your eyes with the twinkly little stars.

- **Hearing**

Listen to soothing or vibrant music - depending on how you feel. If you can, play an instrument to calm your frayed nerves. Close your eyes and absorb the sounds around you mindfully. Ensure you immerse yourself in the sounds of your environment.

- **Touch**

Snuggle under your soft, cozy blanket with your loved one or your snuggly little pet if you have one. Pour a warm cup of coffee and feel the warmth on the mug with your hands before drinking. Make a bubble bath for yourself and take as much time as needed to savor the experience.

- **Smell**

Burn a couple of incense sticks or light up a scented candle. Rub essential oils on the inside of your wrists and inhale deeply. Leave your windows open and let the smell of fresh air wash over you.

- **Taste**

Take your time with dessert after dinner and slow down to enjoy the taste. Mindfully, eat a bowl of ice cream; savor the textures, flavors, and tastes. Don't rush anything; take your time.

You can find more creative ways to use your five senses to self-soothe. If you already have self-care activities that you enjoy, continue practicing them for self-soothing. The more you self-soothe in distressing situations now, the better you'll become at self-soothing in the future.

DISTRACTIONS

In the past, I used to believe that distraction was bad for me. I heard many stories about how dividing my attention can affect my focus and leave me feeling frazzled and scattered. While I found this true, I eventually discovered it doesn't apply to every situation. What exactly does this mean?

Distraction isn't mindlessly watching a movie or replaying a kiss in your head as you try to complete an assigned task with your music player on full blast. No, DBT distraction is purposeful. You're choosing to focus on a particular activity instead of doing what your emotions are urging you to do when you're in a crisis. Acting on your emotions in an emotionally charged situation can only backfire.

Sometimes, detaching from an emotional experience with distractions is good for us. You can use this skill when you are:

- Emotionally overwhelmed
- Have an urge to do something you might later regret
- Feel like you have to solve a problem with urgency

Acting on emotional urges often works against our long-term goals - maintaining stable relationships and self-respect and freeing ourselves of addictive behaviors.

Distract yourself with activities. Do anything that takes your mind off the emotion - clean your closet, declutter your home, play video games, or work out. Just choose an activity that doesn't intensify the negative emotions. You can also do something nice for a loved one or stranger. Refer back to ACCEPTS skill.

Distraction is an effective short-term solution to avoid reacting spontaneously to your emotional urges. Distracting yourself works because it puts a distance between you and the thing upsetting you. It helps until you're calm enough to decide on a proper course of action.

Whether it's anxiety, BPD, or personality disorders, your interactions with people will always be a top concern. Sometimes, these tense interactions can be with your family, friends, or co-workers. Therefore, the following chapter explores how you can use DBT skills to improve your relationships with others.

6

INTERPERSONAL EFFECTIVENESS AND YOUR RELATIONSHIPS

Relationships are like plants. They require certain things to flourish, including healthy roots, stems, air, and water. The more a plant gets these things, the more it grows stronger - it may even bear fruits, depending on its kind. Like plants, your relationships require healthy roots, like a foundation. And they must have the necessary social skills to grow stronger.

However, many of us struggle with building healthy social networks. For example, individuals with BPD find social interactions particularly challenging. So do people on the autism spectrum and others with conditions such as ADHD, depression, and anxiety. These are a few conditions that make building a social network nearly impossible. But they aren't the only reasons why people may struggle with social interactions.

UNDERSTANDING INTERPERSONAL EFFECTIVENESS

DBT interpersonal effective skills allow anyone to build healthy relationships with strong roots. They are specifically designed to help you meet your needs in your relationships while maintaining respect across the board.

Emotional instability can make interpersonal relationships more complicated than they need to be. Even when you form relationships effortlessly, you'll inevitably come to need things from people just as they'll need something from you. As a result, many people struggle to form and maintain healthy relationships.

Your exchanges with others about how they can meet your needs and how you might meet their needs can result in tension, confusion, and conflict. Some of us find it very difficult to ask others for assistance. It's also difficult for some to refuse requests with a firm "No." Learning to handle these situations with ease is a core aspect of interpersonal effectiveness. By mastering the skills, you'll learn to get what you need in a relationship without becoming manipulative or codependent.

How you communicate with others significantly affects the quality of your interpersonal relationships and the outcome of your social interactions. To improve communication, you need interpersonal effectiveness skills to take a more deliberate and thoughtful approach to conversations instead of reacting impulsively to strong emotions or stress.

The two vital skills you'll learn are the ability to ask for your needs to be met and how to say no to people when appropriate. Without these skills, you may find it difficult to state requests or get your needs met, behave appropriately with others, or become vulnerable to exploitation.

Go on the internet right now, and you'll find thousands of books on how you can cultivate the proper skills or a specific skill set for personal development. These books provide a myriad of skills to add to your repertoire to make yourself more appealing to the job market or people around you.

But how do you know which skill is crucial?

It's nearly impossible to answer the above question. Still, I will always tell anyone who cares to hear that interpersonal effectiveness skills are some of the best tools you can have in your social kit.

We meet hundreds of people weekly, and we'll probably meet tens of thousands in one lifetime. You don't necessarily need to impress everyone you encounter by choice or chance. Still, it would be best if you built healthy connections with a reasonable number of them.

Whether you struggle with public speaking, are an extrovert, an introvert, or are just a hermit, there's no reason you shouldn't try to improve your communication skills and enhance your social life. This may seem particularly daunting if you struggle with anxiety, depression, autism, ADHD, or BPD. It's doubly challenging for individuals with these conditions to have adequate social interactions. Fortunately, DBT skills can help hone your interpersonal effectiveness.

Why is interpersonal effectiveness crucial?

Interpersonal effectiveness skills are vital because you need them to:

- Cater to your relationships
- Balance your and others' needs
- Balance your wants and shoulds
- Build and maintain self-respect

To some extent, we all do these things naturally. You're somewhat able to say no or ask for things from others as well. For example, you probably find it easy to say no to more wine on a date, but how easy is it when your codependent friend comes asking for another favor?

The importance of interpersonal effectiveness is reflected in how it's one of the primary modules of DBT - in fact; it's the second module. So, many DBT resources and materials focus on improving a client's interpersonal skills because of it.

But if you're wondering just how crucial interpersonal effectiveness is in DBT, let's discuss that. Remember, earlier in this chapter; I stated that how we communicate with others can impact the quality of our relationships. Well, DBT asserts that interpersonal skills are necessary for this very reason. Because, in turn, the quality of your social interactions and relationships affects your well-being, self-esteem, self-confidence, self-image, and understanding of who you are.

So, you can see just how important it is to have adequate interaction skills. If you think you only need basic effectiveness skills to communicate and you're set, I'd like to say that you're wrong. At one point, I was also comfortable with the skills I already had. But it took mastering communication skills at a high level of effectiveness to realize just how crucial they are.

Like all complex skills, reaching the apex of mastery is practically impossible. In other words, you can never completely master a skill. Even the most accomplished public speakers are not master communicators. So, remember that you can continually improve regardless of your level of mastery.

Numerous studies have shown that improving your interpersonal skills will lead to positive outcomes, especially if you struggle with BPD. More specifically, DBT interpersonal effectiveness skills have improved BPD patients' relationship capabilities and overall symptoms while reducing affective instability.

THE GOALS OF INTERPERSONAL EFFECTIVENESS

Maybe you have these skills but are unsure how to apply them in everyday interactions. Or perhaps you simply don't know the right time to use them. In order to understand which skills are suitable for a specific situation and when to utilize them, you should know the goals of interpersonal effectiveness. And that brings me to the three goals:

- Objective effectiveness
- Relationship effectiveness
- Self-respect effectiveness

Achieving each goal in interactions requires interpersonal skills. Although we can apply some skills in different situations, we need specific skills to accomplish any of the goals.

When working toward achieving an objective, you must be able to clarify what you want from the interaction and identify how to get the results you want. If your interaction goal is relationship effectiveness, then maintaining the relationship is your priority. In that case, you need to determine how meaningful that relationship is to you, what you want from the other person, and the necessary actions you can take to move the relationship forward.

And when your goal is to maintain self-respect, i.e., self-respect effectiveness, you need specific interpersonal skills to help you understand how you would like to feel at the end of the interaction and exactly how to feel like that while sticking to the facts and your values.

In most cases, you'll most likely have at least two goals in a situation. And in others, you may have the three goals. For example, suppose you want to obtain something from your partner, keeping in mind that they're an essential part of your life. In that case, you'll want to maintain your relationship while getting what you want. And you'll likely want to retain self-respect in the asking process and apply the skills for each goal simultaneously.

FACTORS THAT BLOCK INTERPERSONAL EFFECTIVENESS

Several factors can act as obstacles to interpersonal effectiveness if you're already skilled at navigating social interactions. These blocks often arise from time to time, so you must continuously work on developing your interpersonal skills.

No matter the situation or the person involved, when you're experiencing distress, it helps to take a step back and mentally review the situation without judgment. Half of the fight to overcome communication blocks is identifying the real problem, not the one you think it is. This requires taking a long, hard look in the mirror and asking yourself how you might have contributed to the problem.

Usually, we acquire the basics of social interactions from the patterns we see in our families growing up. This means that how you relate with others is most likely modeled after your primary caregiver. Obviously, these patterns aren't always the healthiest or most effective.

As you grow up from childhood to adolescence to adulthood, you gradually enact what you've seen in your families with other people - unhealthy or otherwise. If your parents dealt with conflict using unhealthy techniques, you will likely internalize those techniques and re-enact them in your relationships as an adult.

The good thing is that you can unlearn these patterns; they don't have to continue in adulthood. You're at a point where you can identify these patterns and eliminate them. You can choose much healthier ways of interacting with others.

Below are eight aversive strategies for learning or using interpersonal effectiveness skills.

1. **Discounting:** This is when you communicate your needs by telling the other person that their needs are trivial or invalid. ***Example***: "You've been on your phone all day - do you expect me to clean after you while you just sit around?"
2. **Withdrawing:** Sometimes, you're so afraid that the other person will abandon or withdraw from you that you preemptively withdraw first, emotionally or

in some other way. ***Example***: "You can do anything you want - I'm leaving anyway."

3. **Blaming:** You make everything the other person's fault while absolving yourself of all responsibilities. You tell yourself that they should fix it since they caused it. ***Example***: "We're only in this mess because of you - fix it!"
4. **Threatening:** This happens when you have so much anger inside that you believe the only way to alleviate your pain is to make the other person suffer. ***Example***: "If you don't give me what I want, I will leave you."
5. **Guilt-tripping:** You try to make the other person feel like a failure. Or you make them think they're wrong to ask you to meet their needs. ***Example***: "You wouldn't ask that of me if you cared about me."
6. **Belittling**: You attack others to make them feel wrong, stupid, or defective. ***Example***: "Why did you insist on coming with me? I knew you wouldn't behave appropriately."
7. **Derailing:** This is a strategy to divert attention from the other person's needs or feelings toward yourself and your own needs. ***Example***: "I'm so hurt; I don't care what you say right now."

These are some of the strategies we use to block interpersonal effectiveness. And sometimes, we don't even realize we're doing that.

Other factors that could be blocking interpersonal effectiveness include overthinking or negative thinking, intense emotional arousal, indecision, the environment, and a combination of these factors.

- **Lack of skill**

We tend to dismiss the lack of interpersonal skills as lacking motivation. "I haven't discussed my idea with my boss because I don't want to." But it's probably because you don't know what to say, how to say it, or how to act. If you don't know how to communicate your needs, it won't matter how motivated you are.

Interpersonal skills are acquired the same way we develop other skills: By observing others. You may lack these skills if you don't have anyone to model them for you, you never had the opportunity to observe the skills, or you never had time to practice them.

Like I said earlier, it's possible that you didn't learn healthy interaction skills as a child and, so, have no structure upon which to build them.

- **Overthinking**

Negative thoughts affect our ability to use interpersonal skills. In this case, you have the skills, but you're letting overthinking get in the way of what you want to say or do. "What if my boss doesn't like my idea? I might get fired!"

"I'll end up ruining the task." It's normal to think about potential outcomes for our actions. Still, overthinking makes us hyper-fixate on possible dire consequences. It may push us to worry about being ineffective.

Negative thinking invalidates and creates a cycle of harmful self-talk, making it difficult to achieve our objective in an interaction.

- **Intense emotions**

Emotions are sometimes an automatic response to a situation that has happened in the past, and as you know, emotions impact behavior. In some circumstances, you have the ability to navigate an interaction, but you let your emotions interfere, which causes frustration.

For example, we get frustrated when a situation feels out of control. Or feel guilty because of our reaction to a particular situation.

If you allow them, emotions can become overwhelming and cause you to shut down before or in the interaction process. That's when your distress tolerance skills can aid with interpersonal effectiveness.

- **Indecision**

Negative thinking and intense emotional arousal can cause indecision. This often occurs when we're conflicted about priorities, can't figure out how to balance asking without asking for less or too much, or don't know how to balance saying no or giving in.

In this case, you can't decide what to say or do even though you have the interpersonal skill required.

- **Environment**

In some cases, there could be harmful outcomes to saying no to a request. The other person might take the rejection quite poorly due to their own insecurities, obstructing all chances of salvaging the situation. Sometimes, even those highly skilled at interpersonal interactions simply don't know how to get their way, behave in self-respecting ways, or ensure others continue to like them.

Other times, we consider objective effectiveness, i.e., obtaining our goal, more important than self-respect effectiveness, i.e., retaining our self-respect. In such cases, you'll need radical acceptance to embrace reality as it is.

I mentioned that a combination or interplay of these factors could also block interpersonal effectiveness. The factors play off each other. The more you experience non-giving circumstances (environment), the more you overthink, and the worse you feel. You become stuck in a cycle of ineffectiveness where it becomes impossible to maintain healthy social connections no matter how hard you try.

APPLYING INTERPERSONAL EFFECTIVENESS

There are many things to consider when entering a negotiation with someone else. I use "negotiation" here to refer to the act of asking another person to meet your needs. To successfully use interpersonal effectiveness skills, you must learn how to utilize other DBT skills, including distress tolerance, mindfulness, and emotional regulation.

In interpersonal interactions, we take in a lot of sensory information, such as what the other person says, our physiological responses, thoughts, and present feelings, which are many things to notice and process all at once.

You can only take effective action if you interact with a situation in a mindful manner. Mindfulness is key to interpersonal effectiveness because it allows you to immerse yourself in what's happening so you can notice everything. When you approach your interactions with a mindful attitude, you get too genuinely focus on what's happening.

When I'm about to enter a negotiation, I ask myself a series of questions as a way of utilizing my interpersonal skills. If you learn to ask these questions before making a request of another person or when someone makes a request of you, it'll begin to come naturally. With that in place, you'll be able to make informed decisions on the best way to proceed with negotiations.

Priorities

- How important are my objectives?
- Is this relationship damaged or fragile in any way?
- Am I risking my self-respect?
- Will this interaction injure my self-respect if I refuse this request?

Capability

- Is this person capable of fulfilling my needs?
- Am I capable of giving this person what they want from me?

Timing

- Is this person in the right mood to hear my request?
- When are they most likely to be receptive to my request?
- Is this a good or bad time to turn down their request?

Authority

- Does this person hold authority over me in any way?
- Do I hold authority over them in any way?

Homework

- Am I sufficiently familiar with this request or situation or the person I'm asking for something?
- Do I have the necessary information to present my request to them?
- Am I clear about what I need?
- Am I clear about what the other person is requesting?
- Do I understand what I'm saying yes or committing to?

Rights

- Would accepting this request affect my rights in any way?
- Would turning down this request affect the other person's rights in any way?

Reciprocity

- Have I done as much as I'm asking for this person?
- Have they done as much for me as they're asking for?

Respect

- Do I usually meet my own needs?

- Do I always appear helpless or try to avoid looking helpless?
- Will saying "no" evoke negative feelings about myself?

Long-term vs Short-term

- If I give up on my request right now, will it cause long-term problems later on?
- If I say no to their request, will it cause long-term problems later on?

It's normally impossible for two people in an intimate, platonic, or professional relationship to meet each other's needs every time. Let go of this idea and accept that it's unrealistic. The more realistic thing is that the other person will meet some of your needs most of the time, and vice versa.

When using interpersonal effectiveness skills, think about possible compromises. What are you willing to compromise, and what's non-negotiable? Always find ways to meet the other person halfway to maintain harmony and mutual respect in the relationship.

Combining interpersonal effectiveness with mindfulness practice allows you to attune to your experiences, take a constructive approach to analyzing your thoughts and feelings, and successfully negotiate with the important people in your life.

What should you focus on? Find patterns in how you negotiate with others and determine what needs changing. Don't become overly fixated on fairness in exchanges because that can create a skewed perspective of reality. Also, don't try to be right all the time because that makes it impossible to move forward with harmony and a positive attitude.

Reflect on how attached you are too old communication patterns and take an honest assessment of how you can change your relationships going forward. How would your relationships be different if you gave up on old ways and started approaching interpersonal exchanges with true mindfulness and effectiveness? Change is frightening, but what are you willing to change?

YOUR SOCIAL SKILLS ASSESSMENT

This section has a social skills assessment table to help you understand which areas to work on extensively and which ones need a slight improvement. I recommend taking this assessment as you begin applying the DBT skills you've learned and retaking it a few weeks later.

Rate yourself on the skills below on a scale from 1 to 5 according to the following metric. (don't forget to download your free DBT insider worksheets)

Metric

*In the metric below, 1 means **very bad**, 2 means **bad**, 3 means **occasionally good**, 4 means **usually good**, and 5 means always good.*

1.	I am **very bad** at this skill.
2.	I am **bad** at this skill.
3.	I am **occasionally good** at this skill.
4.	I am **usually good** at this skill.
5.	I am **always good** at this skill.

Here are 20 communication skills to assess yourself.

#	Social Skills	Rating				
1.	Meeting new people	1	2	3	4	5
2.	Introducing yourself	1	2	3	4	5
3.	Listening to I - showing interest in people	1	2	3	4	5
4.	Listening to II - taking in what they say	1	2	3	4	5
5.	Describing your feelings	1	2	3	4	5
6.	Stating your needs	1	2	3	4	5
7.	Dealing with anger, aggression, or hostility	1	2	3	4	5
8.	Receiving praise or criticism	1	2	3	4	5
9.	Receiving negative feedback	1	2	3	4	5
10.	Defusing tension in a conversation	1	2	3	4	5
11.	Increasing the seriousness of a conversation	1	2	3	4	5
12.	Managing silence in a conversation	1	2	3	4	5
13.	Seeking clarification	1	2	3	4	5
14.	Responding to display of apathy or disinterest	1	2	3	4	5
15.	Appreciating people's feelings and needs	1	2	3	4	5
16.	Asking open-ended questions	1	2	3	4	5
17.	Providing relevant information	1	2	3	4	5
18.	Seeking information from others	1	2	3	4	5
19.	Changing the topic or direction of a conversation	1	2	3	4	5
20.	Holding attention or interest	1	2	3	4	5

You can improve this assessment by considering interpersonal communications that aren't included and rating yourself using the above metric. This assessment is an excellent way to figure out where you are and where you want to be.

It's best to use individual values. Still, you can also take the average of all 20 ratings to score an overall "social skill" rating.

To truly improve your interpersonal skills rating, ensure you establish a baseline first. Again, you can do this by taking the assessment at the start of your journey. Creating a baseline gives you something to compare back to. That way, you can observe improvements qualitatively.

The reality is that many of us lack social skills because, in school, our teachers were so preoccupied with teaching algebra, geography, and calculus that they forgot how important it is to acquire practical social skills.

Your interpersonal skills will do more for you than your knowledge of capital cities will do for you - that's a fact. Communication is the most critical aspect of our daily lives as humans because socializing is a priority.

Of course, this isn't to blame the teachers or parents who raised us. Perhaps they lived in a different time when social norms were slightly different. Regardless, you change how you interact and model healthy social skills for the future generation. They'll thank you for it.

In order to learn and model healthy interaction skills for the next generation, it's time to discuss the exact DBT techniques you need in order to improve your interpersonal effectiveness.

7

STRATEGIES TO INCLUDE INTERPERSONAL EFFECTIVENESS IN YOUR LIFE

I once tried learning a new language on Duolingo. After a few weeks, I started to know the basics. I could do greetings and introductions. But there was nobody around me to practice verbally with. Eventually, due to a busy schedule, I had to take time off from Duolingo practice. By the time I returned to learning this language, I had to start all over! Sadly, I couldn't remember what I had learned so far.

Why did this happen? Well, I had no one to speak the language with. So the only place I could practice was on Duolingo. If I had any other way of practicing it while I couldn't use Duolingo, I most likely wouldn't have lost everything I learned.

This is how social skill learning works. You must continuously practice it to remain prolific. Like a language, if you don't regularly practice your social skills, you'll eventually forget or lose them.

There are three key DBT strategies to help you improve interpersonal effectiveness, i.e., boost your social skills. Let's discuss them one by one.

DEAR MAN

DEAR MAN is an interpersonal effectiveness skill for effective communication. This skill will teach you to respectfully express your wants and needs to all parties involved in the interaction, which increases your chances of getting a positive outcome. Using this strategy, you will learn to take a new approach to assertive communication.

The DEAR MAN strategy works specifically for achieving objective effectiveness in an interaction. To get what you want from your relationships and master the ability to react to situations in a non-judgmental manner, DEAR MAN is the fundamental skill to learn and master.

What does the acronym mean?

- **D - Describe**

Describe your situation clearly and without ambiguity. Don't assume that the other person knows what you want to talk about. State it to them in clear terms. Be as factual as possible. You're trying to set up the conversation with facts instead of expressing your feelings outright.

This is important because the other person might not know what you are requesting until you explain it clearly. By laying the facts on the table, you're ensuring they understand the circumstances leading you to make this request.

For example, let's say your spouse has been missing out on many family events due to work. Instead of keeping your discontent to yourself to avoid conflict or lashing out at them, you can communicate and work out a solution together.

You can describe the situation by saying, "I understand that you have a crazy schedule at work which is causing you to miss a lot of commitments at home. I would like us to talk about it."

- **E - Express**

After describing the situation with facts to support it, express how you feel with "I" statements. An "I" statement allows you to be accountable without sending the other person into defense mode. That way, they're unlikely to see your talk as an attack. This is crucial because you want the other person to know how you feel about the situation you've just described to them. It gives them insight into where you're coming from.

Example: *"Because you've never missed commitments so consistently, I'm afraid the kids will feel neglected. I feel that this is the best time for us to be there for them as much as we can. My biggest fear is that your work will cause a divide in the family, and we won't return from it."*

- **A - Assert**

Assert yourself by firmly stating your need or request. To "assert" means to communicate what you want in a clear and strong manner. Depending on the situation, assertiveness could also mean saying a firm "No" to the other person's request. Be direct - don't beat around the bush, make allusions, or leave it up to the other person to guess what you're asking for.

This is important because you're the only one who can read your own mind. Your partner can't, and you shouldn't expect them to. What you want might seem obvious, but the other person might have no idea. Or, they may be unsure exactly what it is you want. Unclear expectations cause significant conflict in many relationships. Remove the ambiguity and lay it on clearly and directly.

Example: *"I want you to make it to the children's parent-teacher conference this Wednesday."*

- **R - Reinforce**

Relationships are all about reciprocity. If someone does you a favor, you're more likely to return that favor. This usually comes naturally. Reinforce what you just started to ensure the other person knows why they must meet that need or grant that request.

Therefore, this reminds the other person that they get something from granting your request or meeting your need, which can help solidify the relationship even more.

Example: *"I appreciate your hard work to keep our finances afloat and how much time you devote to the kids when you get any opportunity. I'll be happy to take over picking up the kids from school on Thursdays."*

- **M - (Be) Mindful**

Stay in the present moment. Don't be distracted by your environment. Instead, commit to the conversation for as long as it goes on. Even if the other person becomes defensive, try your best to stay on course. Distractions come quickly, especially when you have an uncomfortable discussion. But if you let the conversation steer off course, it becomes unlikely that you'd get what you're asking for.

Remain mindful until you both reach a resolution. This will increase the chance of having a successful and productive negotiation.

Example: At this point in the conversation with your spouse, they'll probably have a lot of rebuttals to what you said. It could be about how they're trying their best or how you have a more flexible schedule. Instead of going down that rabbit hole, stay focused on the situation you're addressing.

You might say, *"I understand that you're working hard, and I also acknowledge that I have a more flexible schedule. We can both come up with a better plan to make the kids feel like you're involved in their lives as much as I am."*

- **A - Appear confident**

Forget how you feel on the inside and maintain a confident exterior. Sit upright with your head held high, make direct eye contact, and speak clearly. Being confident signals to the other person that you expect them to grant your request. It becomes hard to turn you down because confidence shows them you aren't making a request that's too difficult to grant.

Example: Appearing confident portrays an air of finality to your spouse. You can display confidence by maintaining eye contact, staying focused on the topic, remaining calm, and stating your request clearly.

- **N - Negotiate**

Remember that the conversation isn't about making a demand. You're asking the other person for something. If they aren't on board, you might have to make compromises. One way you could do that is to alter your request in a way that makes it more appealing to them. Talk to the other person about how you can work together to resolve the problem, and you'll most likely reach a solution together.

Negotiating is meant to show that you're willing to accommodate each other's feelings, needs, and opinions as much as possible. It's a tactic to show that you care about hearing them and can make compromises.

Example: Listen to your spouse and look for a solution that leaves all parties satisfied, including the kids.

The DEAR MAN technique is an excellent skill for communicating and achieving your objective in any interaction, no matter the relationship.

GIVE

"GIVE" is another interpersonal effectiveness skill designed to help improve your communication skills. I always say that some relationships are worth preserving more than others. The GIVE strategy is designed to help you achieve relationship effectiveness.

Interpersonal relationships can be challenging, especially if you struggle to regulate your emotions or control your reactions. As a result, you can easily damage a relationship without even knowing it. GIVE keeps your relationship intact during a conflict or argument. Also, if you have a particular relationship you would like to improve or maintain, this skill can help you do just that.

A considerable part of interpersonal effectiveness is tending to your relationships consistently. Letting hurt and problems accumulate doesn't help. Instead, it's much better to address them as they happen. You can learn this skill to handle issues before they blow up. It's also practical for ending toxic or hopeless relationships.

Please note that you shouldn't continually use the GIVE technique to address issues on undeserving people. It's for relationships that truly matter.

Before beginning an interpersonal interaction for relationship effectiveness, knowing your specific goal is essential. The general goal is to preserve a relationship. But sometimes, you may want the other person to stop criticizing you or perhaps want them to approve of you.

Below are three things to consider before an interaction aimed at improving a relationship:

1. Act in a manner that makes the other person want to grant your request or meet your specific need.

2. Act in a manner that makes the person react positively to you, turning down their request.
3. Balance your immediate goal with what's good for the relationship in the long term.

Ensure that you balance your objective with relationship and self-respect goals. Do not compromise your self-respect for an undeserving person or relationship. Don't grant a request you don't want just to preserve a relationship. All three things highlighted above must be coordinated and balanced effectively.

GIVE is an acronym for:

- **G**entle
- **I**nterested
- **V**alidate
- **E**asy manner

(Be) Gentle

You don't want to come across as threatening or aggressive in communication. It'll only put the other person on the defensive, potentially destroying the relationship you're trying to improve or maintain.

A good part of this skill is to avoid criticizing or denigrating the other person. For example, don't make threats, pass judgment, or attack the other person. You also shouldn't name-call or disrespect them in any way, shape, or form.

Humans are more responsive to gentleness. Being gentle is vital because it's a way to get the other individual to do something you'd like them to do, especially if they just won't do it. Anger and threats may seem like more accessible means to your end. Still, they're unlikely to help you achieve the goal of relationship effectiveness. Instead, be open to taking "no" for an answer.

Approach the conversation assuming the other person has reasons for their actions, opinions, or decisions. Even if you disagree with them, it's not a call to disrespect them. Instead, ensure your facial expressions and body language convey respect and your language and actions.

Give the other person time and space to come up with a response. If they request postponing or delaying the conversation or having it in a safer space, accept it and move forward.

(Act) Interested

You feel awful when trying to talk to someone, but they appear more interested in something else, like their phone. It's pretty hurtful, so you shouldn't do it to another person. Instead, when someone is communicating with you, the only right thing to do is listen to them. Show interest in their point of view. No matter how challenging it is, act interested in the conversation - even if it is dreadfully dull.

Humans respond well to interest from the person they're interacting with. So it's okay to wonder if acting interested is dishonest - it isn't. Remember that you're trying to have a pleasant conversation and maintain or improve your relationship with the other person. You can't let disinterest get in the way of that.

Acting interested helps you achieve the relationship effectiveness goal. At some point, you may even find that you're genuinely interested in the conversation. So, maintain direct eye contact, nod occasionally, and let your facial expressions portray interest.

The results may be easier than you think.

Validate

This skill shows the other person that you listened to and understood everything they said. You do this with words and actions. Express that you understand their perspective and why they would feel the way they do. You can validate a person's opinions, feelings, or actions without agreeing with them. Validating doesn't necessarily indicate agreement.

For example, let's say you're upset at your friend for canceling your lunch plans at the last minute. Perhaps he gave an excuse that something came up at work, but you aren't convinced it warranted canceling your plans.

In that case, you may respond with, "I'm sorry something came up at work, and I know how hard you work." Notice that this response doesn't address the problem. This is an excellent example of how to validate, and it's great for maintaining relationships you want to give a second chance.

This skill is handy during disagreements. It teaches you to be more understanding of other people's perspectives, opinions, feelings, etc. Even if you already have a strong relationship, validating can strengthen it.

Easy manner

Smile. Be grateful. Find humor in the situation and throw that into the conversation. Don't make the conversation tense or painful because that will only strain the relationship. Using an easy manner in the interaction allows you to counter potential strains or tensions.

It doesn't matter if you disagree with the other person. However, you shouldn't let the conversation turn sour or adversarial. Instead, make it as light and easy-going as possible. You'll find that soothes the tension.

Nobody wants to feel like another person is guilt-tripping, threatening, or pushing them around. So don't be a bully.

A good attitude increases your chances of getting what you want. However, it can be hard to maintain an easy manner when the other person goes on the defensive or feels hurt by your request. Just remember that their feelings are valid. Try to keep a calm and easy manner as you accept their response or reaction.

Before I use the GIVE skill, I like to think of how I would like other people to treat me during a similar discussion or argument. For example, do I want to be yelled at or spoken to softly? What would either approach look like in words and actions?

Then, I take my answers and use them to practice having the discussion. You can practice with a trusted friend or your adorable pet; ensure you utilize all the tips and tricks given here. Also, don't wait until you have a serious discussion to use these skills. It's easier to remember them if you regularly utilize them.

The DBT GIVE skill is another valuable tool to improve social skills and interactions. Don't forget to put it into practice!

FAST

The "FAST" strategy helps achieve self-respect effectiveness during communication. A long time ago, I embodied passivity; by default, the communication type was passive communication. I tried my best to avoid difficult conversations and conflicts, even at a high personal cost. I never put my needs first; in fact, I often rehearsed things I'd say and how I'd say them to my partner, parents, boss, siblings, or friends, but once the conversation got too intense, I would stay away.

I quite literally felt my self-respect fading away. Thankfully, I became familiar with DBT and learned to shed passive communication for assertive communication. I have learned how to keep self-respect during a disagreement or conflict using the FAST skill, and I want you to do the same.

FAST is an acronym that outlines subskills for maintaining self-respect when trying to get another person to meet your needs.

- **F - Fair**

Be fair, both to yourself and the other person. Fair represents being tactfully honest about your needs and those of the person you're interacting with. It opens up a path to constructive and productive criticism, allowing you to preserve the relationship as you want.

Expressing your needs instead of hiding them or covertly hinting at them requires a degree of assertiveness, which is what "fair" helps you achieve. Being fair also means treating the other person how you would like to be treated.

- **A - No Apologies**

Unnecessary apologies are a no-no. You should only apologize if you've indeed done something that requires apologizing. That is key to rebuilding trust and repairing a damaged relationship. However, if you've done nothing to be sorry for, there's no need to apologize compulsively. You might surprise yourself if you decide to consciously take note of how often you apologize in a day.

Remember that apologizing for mistakes that aren't yours only instills an unnecessary sense of guilt.

- **S - Stick to your values**

The urge to compromise your values to please the other person is usually incredibly high during a conflict. So naturally, you want to please the other person. But don't forget that you also want to keep self-respect, so you mustn't forget what's important to you.

Before the interaction, make a list of your values and explore them. That way, you can decide which values are non-negotiable. You shouldn't have to lose your values to gain the other individual's approval. In fact, if they cannot respect your values, it might be time to reevaluate your relationship with them.

Sticking to your values can help achieve successful conflict resolution.

- **Truthful**

Being truthful means avoiding lies, excuses, and exaggerations. It includes being accountable for your actions while recognizing how to differentiate another person's actions from yours during a conflict.

By demonstrating accountability, you can view your role in the situation from a more authentic point of view. That can help decrease anxiety as you reflect on your actions. But, more importantly, it enables you to identify the areas you can improve on.

Try the FAST skill the next time you find yourself in a conflict and see how it goes.

THINK

Usually, when we have a conflict with another person, we approach the interaction with a negative attitude. This is because your brain naturally interprets the person's words or actions as threatening or attacking. So, you jump to conclusions, causing you to lash out and become defensive or hostile.

Emotions like anger or frustration can make it difficult to control your actions in a tense situation. This defeats your goal of achieving interpersonal effectiveness, especially if you want to improve a relationship, maintain self-respect, or communicate more healthily and productively.

Luckily, the DBT THINK skill can help you reduce conflict and disagreements. You can use this skill to enter the Wise mind, where you can constructively resolve conflicts.

- **T - Think**

Think about the conflict or situation from the other person's point of view. How might they interpret your words, actions, and situation? In other words, put yourself in the person's shoes and think about their perspective.

- **H - Have empathy**

How might the other person be feeling? Are they angry? Sad? Frustrated? Stressed? Anxious? Uncomfortable? It's important to empathize and consider their feelings during the conversation.

- **I - Interpret**

Can you interpret the person's actions in more than one way? Is there an alternate explanation for their behavior? Ensure you seek at least one positive interpretation of the cause of the conflict. That allows you to maintain a productive attitude during the interaction.

- **N - Notice**

Pay attention to how the other person might have been trying to improve or salvage the situation. How are they showing that they care? What skills are they applying to the situation? Are they struggling with stressors or personal problems?

Notice how these affect their behavior in the present moment.

- **K - (Be) Kind**

Treat the other person how you would want them to treat you in a similar situation. Remain kind and gentle during the interaction. Don't allow powerful emotions or a negative attitude to cloud your judgment during conflict resolution. Instead, pair the THINK, GIVE, FAST, and DEAR MAN skills to develop and maintain healthy relationships with people.

THE IMPORTANCE OF ASSERTIVE COMMUNICATION

Assertiveness is a vital communication skill. It allows you to express yourself more effectively and confidently. More importantly, it helps you do this while respecting other people's beliefs or opinions. Assertive communication can also help cope with stress and anger more productively.

Being assertive can help you:

- Boost self-esteem and self-confidence
- Recognize and understand feelings

- Achieve mutual respect
- Enhance decision-making
- Build honest relationships

You can be more assertive in conversations by:

- Using "I" statements.
- Learning to say "No."
- Keeping your emotions in check

Becoming an assertive communicator takes time and practice. Learning assertiveness may take a while if you've spent years expressing yourself passively. But you'll get there as long as you put in the work.

HEALTHY BOUNDARY-SETTING

Setting healthy personal boundaries is the key to avoiding many arguments, disagreements, and conflicts that lead to stress. The absence of boundaries undermines your identity, values, and beliefs. It ultimately undervalues your true sense of self.

If other people's treatment of you often triggers you, it's time to set healthy emotional and physical boundaries. Boundaries are a measure of self-image and self-esteem. They let people know what you consider acceptable and unacceptable.

How do you do this?

- Write down how important each person in your personal or professional life affects your feelings, mood, etc. Then, think about the motivations behind their behavior.
- Decide on a specific course of action. For example, you may decide to start saying "No" when your boss asks you to stay behind late.
- Write down five things you'd like each person to stop doing to you and around you. For example, you may want your partner to stop ignoring you.
- Write down five things you will no longer allow each person to say to you.

Reevaluate your current boundaries and update them as necessary. Also, be sure to update the new boundaries from time to time. Sometimes, they become invalid.

Establish strong personal boundaries, and people will give you the respect you deserve. The best thing about setting healthy boundaries is it allows you to be your authentic self.

The final step is like the final piece of the puzzle that will help bring all steps together. Our impulses, fears, anger, mood swings, chronic boredom, and self-image all boil down to how we regulate our emotions.

8

THE POWER OF EMOTIONAL REGULATION

Emotions are mystifying! At some point, we've all been interrupted by some intense emotion, like anger, frustration, or inadequacy, for no apparent reason. That's because our underlying beliefs about emotions affect our ability to regulate and control them when they arise.

This is made even more complex by the beliefs we have about emotions. For example, certain people believe emotions are either positive or negative; some argue that they are a manageable force; and some view emotions, particularly negative ones, as undesired interlopers that corrupt our psyche.

Many of these beliefs are subconscious, meaning we aren't aware of them. We form them based on our experiences and the explicit and implicit messages society passes to us.

However, new research has revealed that these beliefs are false or grossly misrepresented. Yet, they impact our behavior in significant ways.

Contrary to popular belief, emotions are neither good nor bad, controllable or uncontrollable, positive or negative. Every emotion is felt for a reason - to alert you of something you aren't paying attention to.

Your ability to regulate emotions and control your responses to them will determine your perception of those emotions. After all, this will ultimately set the foundation for a positive or negative outcome, which is the most important thing.

Imagine that your old friend ignores your invitation to a lunch date after being away for a long time. Naturally, you'd be upset, disappointed, or angry. But if you don't submit to the emotion you're experiencing and instead think about the situation from a different perspective - maybe your friend didn't get the email or the text you sent, or they're just busy with more important things - that would help you regulate your emotions and stop you from acting out in a way you'd regret.

This ability to control how you think about and respond to emotions is called "Emotion Regulation." It is tied to many positive health benefits, including moral decision-making, improved mental health, memory, and general well-being.

Understanding Emotion Regulation

Before discussing emotion regulation, I noticed that many people confuse it with emotional intelligence. As you may already know, emotional intelligence is the ability to understand and manage your emotions.

Therefore, it is similar to emotion regulation. The difference is, that emotion regulation is a subset of emotional intelligence, which is more than the ability to control emotions.

Emotional intelligence is *"the ability to recognize, manage, and understand emotions. It includes the ability to recognize, interpret, and regulate your own emotions and those of others."*

Daniel Goleman, a psychologist who popularized the concept of emotional intelligence, introduced five components of emotional intelligence.

The five critical components of emotional intelligence are:

1. Self-awareness

This is your ability to recognize and understand your emotions. It's one of the critical skills everyone must possess. After all, how can you regulate an emotion you aren't even aware of?

Self-awareness involves:

- Monitoring your emotions.
- Becoming aware of your emotional triggers and reactions.
- Correctly identifying each emotion, you experience.

2. Social skills

Interacting effectively with others is another critical component of emotional intelligence. As you've learned, you need strong social skills to build meaningful emotional connections and relationships with other people. Without this skill, you will live a lonely life.

3. Empathy

Understanding others' feelings is a vital aspect of emotional intelligence. But it goes beyond the ability to identify people's emotional states. Empathy entails how you respond to people based on your knowledge of their emotional state. For example, when you sense that someone is grieving, how do you respond to them?

4. Motivation

Intrinsic motivation comes from within. It is the ability to get motivated by things other than fame, money, accolades, or recognition. Instead, you're driven by a passion for fulfilling your goals and innate needs.

5. Self-regulation

Typically, this comes after self-awareness, but I decided to put it last because it's our focus in this chapter. Awareness of and understanding your emotions isn't enough - you must know how to manage and regulate them.

When people hear self-regulation, they think it's about hiding their feelings away or putting them on lockdown. This is one of the common misconceptions about "negative" feelings - we believe we must suppress them.

On the contrary, self-regulation is about finding the right time and place to express your feelings. Emotion regulation is about suppressing your emotions until you can properly express them.

Once you properly train yourself to regulate your emotions, you become flexible and adaptive to change. You also become better at managing difficult or tense situations and resolving conflict if you cannot avoid it.

The more skilled you are in emotion regulation, the more conscientious you become. In other words, you take responsibility for your actions and become more thoughtful about how your words, actions, and behavior influence others.

EMOTIONAL REGULATION VS. EMOTIONAL DYSREGULATION

While emotions are a regular and constant part of everyday life, some people experience more volatile and intense emotions than the average person. And these higher highs and lower lows subsequently begin to affect their lives.

If you experience volatile emotions, you may feel happy at this moment and intensely sad the next. While we all have occasional periods where our emotions spiral out of control, some people experience this more regularly than others.

Often, the rapidly changing emotions cause them to misbehave, i.e., they say and do things they later regret. Unfortunately, that hurts their credibility and damages their personal and professional relationships.

I defined emotional regulation earlier, but this time, let's look at a more in-depth and academic definition.

"Emotional regulation refers to the process by which individuals influence which emotions they have, when they have them, and how they experience and express their feelings. Emotional regulation can be automated or controlled, conscious or unconscious. It may affect one or more points in the emotion-producing process."

From this definition, it is apparent that emotional regulation is a complex process that involves the ability to initiate, inhibit, and modulate your cognitive state and behavior in response to an internal or external event (trigger).

First, an internal or external stimulus (thinking about a crush or a personal loss) triggers an objective effect, i.e., feeling or emotion. Second, it provokes a cognitive response, i.e., thought, accompanied by an emotion-based physiological response (such as increased heart rate). Finally, a related behavior (expression, avoidance, or physical action) follows.

Emotional regulation is the ability to keep these processes within a socially acceptable proportion. In contrast, emotional dysregulation is the exact opposite of this. It is the inability to control or manage your emotional response to a triggering event or stimuli. With the right emotional triggers, anyone can become emotionally dysregulated.

However, individuals with a history of psychological trauma tend to have multiple triggers; Plus, emotional dysregulation is typically prolonged in some people, resulting in significant rifts in daily functioning and relationships. Emotional dysregulation is also associated with chronic stress, anxiety, and depression.

When an individual experiences prolonged emotional dysregulation, they may react exaggeratedly to environmental and interpersonal emotion-based triggers. For example, they may display intense bursts of anger, cry, create conflict, or exhibit passive-aggressive behavior.

If you find it challenging to regulate your emotions, being in an upsetting situation will cause strongly felt emotions that you won't recover from so quickly. For instance, a simple argument with a friend or family member may invoke such strong emotions that you overreact to the situation in a way that significantly impacts your relationship with the person.

On a national level, you probably know it's time to let go of the unfortunate incident. Still, emotionally, you can't control how strongly you feel about it. You can't stop thinking about what happened, causing you to lose sleep and interest in other things.

That inevitably pushes you to escalate the conflict until your relationship is damaged and difficult to repair. Then, in an extreme scenario, you may turn to substance use to improve how you feel about yourself, thus creating more problems instead of solving the ones on the ground.

Emotional dysregulation has long been identified as a symptom of traumatic disorders. One of the things that may trigger emotional dysregulation is maltreatment in childhood which often leads to Post Traumatic Stress Disorder (PTSD). In addition, there is robust evidence linking childhood interpersonal trauma with emotional dysregulation.

You should know that nobody is born with emotional regulation skills. A newborn baby is incapable of self-soothing due to biological immaturity. It is developed. The infant must have a healthy, nurturing relationship with its primary caregiver in order to develop.

As infants grow, they acquire emotional regulation skills from important adults, including parents, teachers, and close family members. For example, the father or mother may teach the child helpful ways to seek solutions to a problem instead of becoming overwhelmed in the face of challenges.

In contrast, kids with traumatic upbringings, especially those raised by parents with PTSD, cannot learn emotion regulation skills. A traumatized parent or caregiver cannot control their own emotions; therefore, they are unlikely to be able to teach their child.

Sometimes, the traumatized parent may even escalate their child's distress with outbursts or disproportionate emotional responses to the child's problems. In such cases, the child cannot learn vital emotion regulation skills.

Emotional dysregulation is associated with PTSD, BPD, ADHD, Substance abuse, Bipolar Disorder, Disruptive Mood Dysregulation Disorder, and Autism Spectrum Disorders. As you already know, emotional dysregulation makes building healthy, long-lasting interpersonal relationships challenging.

The general idea of emotion dysregulation is that you experience overly intense emotions compared to the event or stimuli that triggered them. This encompasses a range of reactions from being unable to self-soothe or calm down to suppressing difficult emotions or hyper-fixating on the negative. Individuals with emotion dysregulation also behave erratically, irrationally, and impulsively when their emotions are out of control.

Let's look at more examples of emotion dysregulation.

- Your spouse cancels dinner plans, and you conclude that they no longer want you in their life. So, you stay up all night crying and feeding on junk.
- Your waiter at the local restaurant doesn't attend to your order on time. So, you have an angry outburst and fling the tray across the room when they finally bring your meal.
- You attend your firm's luncheon, where everyone except you seems to have the time of their lives. You feel like an outsider because you can't participate in the conversations. After the luncheon, you go home and have a binge-eating session to numb your hurt.

Emotional dysregulation can also make it challenging to recognize the emotion you're experiencing during an intense emotional reaction. You may feel confused, guilty, or overwhelmed due to the emotion. This can make it nearly impossible to make decisions or manage your actions.

Emotional dysregulation in kids may manifest differently, involving crying, outbursts, temper tantrums, refusing to speak or make eye contact, etc.

The inability to manage your emotional reactions impacts your behavior negatively, which, in turn, affects your adult life in the following ways.

- You have difficulty sleeping.
- You hold grudges longer than necessary because you can't seem to let go of past experiences.
- You find yourself in minor disagreements that you exaggerate and blow out of proportion.
- You experience a negative impact on your social functioning, work, school, etc.

In extreme cases, being unable to regulate your emotions leads to addiction or substance abuse problems. It may also cause you to engage in self-harm, binge-eating, restrictive eating, and other harmful behaviors.

Emotional dysregulation is a normal part of the human experience. As I explained earlier, we all experience some degree of dysregulation regarding our emotions. We also exhibit dysregulated behavior from time to time.

However, the prognosis for individuals who frequently experience emotional dysregulation depends on how severe the underlying issue is. Regardless of the underlying psychological problem, DBT addresses most issues associated with emotional dysregulation and can help anyone learn to regulate their emotions better.

KNOW YOUR EMOTIONAL TRIGGERS

Every day, you experience a range of emotions - joy, excitement, frustration, unease, disappointment, and several others. Every emotion you feel relates to a specific event, such as seeing your adorable pet, having dinner with a romantic interest, talking to your boss, or discussing current events with an acquaintance. Usually, your responses to each emotional experience will vary based on your mindset, attitude, and the underlying context of the situation.

Emotional triggers could be anything - such as experiences, memories, or current events - that evokes strong emotional reactions to a situation regardless of your mood at that particular moment. These triggers are typically linked to PTSD.

Everyone has different emotional triggers. Knowing your emotional triggers is key to being emotionally aware. It's crucial to know your triggers and how to cope with them. Please do not overlook this, as it is essential for optimal emotional and physical health.

Emotional triggers look different from individual to individual, and just about everyone has them. For example, some people appreciate constructive criticism and feedback, while others feel slighted by them. While you might laugh at an embarrassing situation and make a joke, another person might feel entirely ashamed.

Your emotional triggers might be associated with unwanted memories, distressing topics, your habits, or someone else's words or actions. Below are situations that typically trigger intense emotional reactions:

- Betrayal
- Rejection
- Challenged beliefs
- Helplessness
- Unfair treatment
- Criticism or disapproval
- Insecurity
- Being ignored or excluded
- Dependence or loss of independence
- Feeling unwanted or unneeded
- Feeling smothered

These are generic emotional triggers. Some triggers are specific to each person, so how do you figure out your emotional triggers?

- **Listen to your body and mind**

To learn your emotional triggers, you must start by paying attention to your mind and body. Notice when a situation evokes an intense emotional response. Next, be aware of the physiological symptoms that often accompany strong emotions: increased heart rate, sweaty palms, dizziness or shakiness, upset stomach, etc.

- **Take a step back**

When you notice the surging emotion and the accompanying symptoms, take a step back from the situation that triggered them. Use that moment to consider what happened and why it activated that particular emotional response.

Say you spent the entire day decluttering your home and rearranging everything to make it more aesthetic. When you finish, you feel satisfied and wait excitedly for your lover to get home and see what you've done. But instead, they return home and go straight to the kitchen for a drink and then settle on the couch to see a TV show without uttering a single comment about the new look of your home.

Naturally, you feel disappointed they didn't acknowledge your hard work, and you feel frustration and anger rising. You can feel your heart racing and your jaws getting clenched. You had to muster everything to stop yourself from snapping and saying something like, "How stupid can you be? Notice anything different about this house?"

- **Trace the origin**

Follow your feelings back to their roots by reflecting on the situation that triggered them. Perhaps you suddenly felt like that teenager that did everything to gain her mother's approval again, without ever getting it.

The emotional trigger here is your partner's indifference toward your effort. When that trigger fired, you felt transported back to a certain point in childhood, when nothing you did was considered good enough.

- **Be curious**

Sometimes, connecting a trigger and the emotion it evoked is difficult. In that case, you have to let curiosity take over and dig a little bit deeper. When you experience intense, overwhelming emotions, don't suppress or ignore them. Instead, use curiosity to get a deeper insight into what triggered them.

Watch out for any patterns. For instance, discussions about romantic relationships might trigger frustration relating to your fear of abandonment.

Once you've learned to identify your emotional triggers, the next step is to know how to manage them.

MANAGE YOUR EMOTIONAL TRIGGERS

Usually, once people can identify their triggers, they think that the solution is to avoid the situations that may fire those triggers. Sadly, it's not as easy as that. Avoiding or escaping from every situation that may evoke difficult emotions is impossible. You're guaranteed to experience unwanted emotions from time to time. Thus, your best step would be to learn how to prepare for and deal with triggers that might arise in your daily life.

Here are some pointers to help you:

- **Own your emotions**

First, you must acknowledge that it's okay to have these feelings - sad, frustrated, angry, or envious. No matter how unpleasant the emotion is, it's normal for triggers to evoke it. I noticed that reminding myself of the difference between the past and the present often helps with embracing my emotions. You can do this with compassion and without judgment.

- **Take a break**

Sometimes, we need physical space to avoid overwhelming emotions. So, take a break - put some distance between you and the situation that triggered your emotions. This should help you avoid impulsively doing something you'd regret later.

Once alone, you can do some breathing or grounding exercises we discussed in a previous chapter. Plus, you'll find more exercises in the chapter after this.

The goal is to delay your reaction to the situation to a more appropriate time when you can handle it productively.

- **Keep an open mind**

In most cases, people in our lives don't set out trying to make us feel bad. Some words and actions that upset you are a byproduct of the other person's emotional triggers and other underlying factors.

When your partner walked in without realizing you'd transformed the home, it could be because they had a hard day at work or received some bad news that made them want to decompress first.

Everyone has their own underlying emotions at all times, and you won't know what's going on with them until you talk about it. It's easier to understand a person's action or behavior when you purposefully seek out a different perspective. .

DEVELOPING EMOTIONAL SELF-AWARENESS

Emotional awareness isn't something you're born with - it's a skill you can learn with practice, patience, and diligence. You learn and develop emotional awareness by knowing how to tune in to difficult emotions and manage them without getting overwhelmed.

The thing about emotions is that they are always there, bubbling beneath the surface, whether you're consciously aware of them or not. They influence your thinking and everything you do, even if you don't realize it.

Emotional awareness is a skill that helps you understand your feelings and why you have those feelings. It is being able to recognize and express what you're feeling to yourself or other people. More importantly, it is finding the connection between that feeling and a resulting action or behavior.

But as I said earlier, emotional awareness is more than just knowing your emotions. It also entails being able to recognize and understand other people's feelings. Again, emotional awareness encompasses two core subskills:

- The ability to recognize and label your emotional experiences.
- The ability to regulate and manage your emotional experiences without getting overwhelmed.

Why does emotional awareness matter?

Instinctive emotional reactions to a trigger typically happen due to a lack of emotional awareness. When you have an outburst, it's usually because you couldn't feel the physiological signs of that emotion rising internally.

Your feelings drive your actions (behavior). A lack of awareness of your feelings culminates in a lack of understanding of your behavior. This results in the inability to appropriately manage that behavior or accurately determine others' wants and needs.

Becoming emotionally aware means you know how to:

- Recognize who you are, how you feel, what you don't like, and what you need and don't need.
- Understand and empathize with other people's feelings and needs.
- Express your feelings and needs effectively.
- Make informed decisions relating to the most important things to you.
- Motivate yourself and take action to achieve your goals.
- Build healthy, long-lasting emotional connections.

Developing emotional awareness can help you create a balance in life. We sometimes think that life is about high highs and low lows. Emotional awareness can moderate the ups and downs, thus striking a necessary balance. If you often end up in situations you regret, becoming emotionally aware can save you from yourself.

Nowadays, it's hard to build new relationships. But you can meet more people and create new, long-lasting bonds if you train yourself to become more emotionally aware than you are currently.

Of course, to become more emotionally aware, you must evaluate your current emotional awareness.

- How many strong emotions can you tolerate, including positive and negative ones?
- Can you feel physical sensations relating to a strong emotion in your body?
- Do you make decisions impulsively or based on instinct?
- Are you comfortable with every emotion you experience?
- Do you find it hard to talk about your emotions - particularly the unpleasant ones?
- Are you comfortable with people being aware of how you feel?
- Are you able to empathize with others' feelings? How easy can you pick up on someone else's feelings without them talking to you?

Answer these questions honestly. Even if you didn't answer "always" or "usually" or "sometimes" to most of them, know that you aren't alone.

The first place to start is to learn to manage stress. The best way to develop or increase emotional awareness is to become friends with all of your emotions and their physical signs. Once you know how to do this, identifying and managing other emotions become much easier.

Emotional awareness is defined by your ability to relieve stress instantly, which is at the core of many unpleasant emotions. Learn how to de-stress and calm yourself down using the DBT techniques we discussed in the last two chapters, and you can begin to explore frightening or disagreeable emotions.

In the final chapter, I will discuss how you can manage and regulate your emotions with Vagus Nerve Stimulation (VNS) and other beneficial techniques.

9

EXERCISES TO REGULATE AND MANAGE YOUR POWERFUL EMOTIONS

In chapter four, I explained how you could use techniques such as singing, breathing exercises, and massage to stimulate the vagus nerve and soothe agitated emotions at any moment. However, these techniques aren't the only ways to encourage vagus nerve stimulation. There are other ways we'll be focusing on, along with other excellent techniques for mastering, regulating, and managing your emotions.

So far, you have learned that DBT entails four practical steps. But one thing to keep in mind about all four steps to DBT is that they are all interconnected. There is no clear line separating them. Think of DBT as a dish and these four steps as the different parts of the recipe - you need all four to make it a success.

Mindfulness, vagus nerve stimulation, distress tolerance skills, etc., are all excellent reasons for DBT making a great treatment option for different conditions due to its wide range of benefits.

Remember, techniques like STOP can help you navigate a distressing situation or take a step back from intense emotions even when there isn't an immediate crisis.

In the previous chapter, when we looked at how you can return the body to a calm state with various techniques, including vagus nerve stimulation, I mentioned that there is a connection between this nerve and the gut.

And unsurprisingly, how you treat your gut impacts the vagus nerve. So let's briefly examine how probiotics affect the vagus nerve to understand this.

LONG-TERM STIMULATION OF THE VAGUS NERVE

The vagus nerve is the most significant link between the brain and the gastrointestinal tract. This relationship is labeled "the brain-gut axis" by scientists. As you know, activation of the vagus nerve plays a crucial role in influencing the parasympathetic nervous system - including the fight or flight response, digestion, immune function, heart rate, and mood.

Due to this connection between the gut and brain, the vagus nerve can modulate various mental health conditions such as anxiety, depression, PTSD, and others. Research shows that these psychiatric conditions are linked to inflammation and gastrointestinal problems.

Eating probiotics can impart various health benefits. The gut-brain axis is a vital relationship that is furthered with the help of probiotics. Gut bacteria impact brain health; therefore, you can improve brain health by changing your gut bacteria. However, there are varying types of probiotics.

Psychobiotics are probiotics that specifically affect the brain. Some have been proven to improve acute or chronic stress, anxiety, and depression symptoms. In fact, a small study involving people with irritable bowel syndrome and mild depression discovered that symptoms improved using a probiotic called Bifidobacterium longum NCC3001.

This shows that probiotics can be quite helpful in achieving vagus nerve stimulation. As gut bacteria ferment probiotics, they can improve brain health and positively impact conditions relating to brain health.

Another study on the link between probiotics and the cortisol response found that a probiotic called Galacto-oligosaccharides significantly reduced the production of cortisol when taken for three weeks. Cortisol is the body's stress hormone responsible for the stress response, which sometimes induces emotion dysregulation.

Taking probiotics can reduce the stress response, making it easier to regulate your emotions whenever you want to. It's much easier to return the body to a calm state when your cortisol level isn't unreasonably high.

Apart from probiotics, many foods are beneficial to the gut-brain relationship. Introducing more of the following foods into your dietary routine will make a significant difference.

- **Omega-3 fats**: These fats abound in high quantities in the brain but are also available in oily fish. Eating more fish with omega-3 fats can increase the fermentation of good bacteria in your gut.
- **High-fiber food**: Nuts, seeds, whole grains, fruits, vegetables, etc., are all foods with high levels of prebiotic fibers that can help increase healthy gut bacteria.
- **Fermented food**: Yogurt, cheese, sauerkraut, and kefir are fermented foods that can alter brain health and activity. This is due to these foods' healthy microbes - such as lactic acid bacteria.

You can make vagus nerve stimulation much easier if you change the type of bacteria fermented in your gut by changing what you eat or eating more probiotics. Anything that benefits your gut health also benefits your brain health.

LABEL YOUR EMOTION

Earlier, we discussed the necessity of emotional awareness - how you need to be able to identify and label the emotions you're experiencing in order to change or regulate them. Everyone experiences six primary emotions - sadness, fear, anger, joy, disgust, and surprise. Then, we also experience secondary and tertiary emotions.

Primary emotions are the underlying reason for any secondary or tertiary emotion you experience. Sometimes, when we say "I'm tired," it could mean that we're sad, depressed, bored, or lonely. Emotions are interconnected. To accurately label whatever you're feeling in a particular moment, you must figure out the primary emotion underlying it. Questions are necessary if you want to label your emotions accurately.

The following is a seven-step process for identifying and labeling your emotions.

1. Trigger (Prompting Event)

Emotions are reactions to an internal or external event - something that happened within you or in your immediate environment. The event that prompts your emotion is called a trigger, as you learned in the previous chapter. A trigger calls forth emotions, which could be anything from your thoughts, behavior, and physical reactions to another person's behavior or actions. Sometimes, we have intuitive feelings that aren't prompted by any thoughts.

Labeling your emotion requires analyzing the prompting event. It could be an interaction with someone, a loss, financial problems, physical illness, or anything happening to you in the present. It could also be a memory of a past event, a thought, or an underlying feeling (feeling ashamed can prompt anger or rage).

When regulating your emotions, you must be able to recognize the prompting event.

2. Interpretation of the prompting event

Usually, it's not an event itself that prompts a particular emotion. Instead, it's the interpretation of the event that triggers a distressing emotion. The feelings arise after we interpret the event through a specific viewpoint. In other words, the explanation you give for why the event happened causes the rise of negative feelings.

For example, say you see your girlfriend and her male friend laughing together. You immediately conclude that there's something more than a platonic friendship between them. And so, you feel jealousy and anger well up within you.

Or maybe you ended up staying at work later than usual. Then, on your way home, there is a storm, and you feel fear rising within you because you've heard of people getting struck to death by lightning.

Different events can result in the same emotion based on interpretation. Remember that how you interpret a prompting event is determined by many factors, which aren't always factual. Your interpretation may be valid, but that doesn't make it a fact.

3. Physiological response to emotion

I previously explained that the body experiences physiological changes when emotions rise. Unfortunately, many people struggle with noticing these physical sensations. To label an emotion, you have to become pretty good at identifying the physical changes that accompany it.

Emotions often involve physical changes such as relaxing or tensing muscles, rise and drop in blood pressure, and changes in breathing, heart rate, skin color, and temperature.

The changes you want to pay attention to happen in the facial area are:

- Tightened cheeks
- Tightening muscles around the eyes
- Clenched jaws
- Grinding teeth
- Tight forehead muscles

Notice your facial expressions and posture. They are minor changes but can tell you much about your feelings.

4. Urges

Triggers prompt emotions, which prompts behaviors. One function of emotions is to urge us to take action, i.e., behave in a specific way. For example, when you're angry, you get the urge to confront or fight the object of your anger. Or when you feel afraid, you're prompted to run or fight.

A resulting action isn't part of the emotion that prompted it. Still, the urge to engage in that action or behavior is part of the emotional process. For example, when you're angry, you will feel the urge to yell or scream at the person who made you angry.

That urge is part of the feeling, but whatever action you take isn't included in the emotional process.

5. Expressing the emotion

Emotions are your brain's way of communicating with your body. So, emotions are meant to be expressed. Often, we struggle with expressing our emotions. Even when we think we're communicating how we feel, the other person may not understand, which may result in misunderstandings

To accurately label an emotion, you must express precisely how you feel. We communicate our feelings through words, actions, and facial expressions. However, communicating emotions through behavior sometimes causes misunderstandings because behavior is subject to interpretation, like emotional triggers.

6. Name the emotion

If you're not accustomed to labeling your emotions, the first time will be challenging. But, thankfully, you can become good at it with practice.

Many variables interfere with your ability to observe, describe, and name emotions. Secondary emotions are one of these variables.

For example, anger comes after shame. Maybe you found yourself in an embarrassing situation. After the initial feeling of shame, you become angry at yourself for getting in that situation in the first place.

Some feel multiple emotions at the same time - that's quite natural. For example, you may feel sad and angry at the same time if the situation warrants it. The secondary emotion makes it challenging to figure out the underlying feeling, making the emotion harder to deal with.

Always unravel your primary and secondary emotions so you can name them.

7. After Effects

Again, emotions, thoughts, and behaviors exist in a cycle - they affect each other and, together, affect physical function. Sometimes, the after-effects of an emotional experience last longer. One unfortunate after-effect is that a prompting event triggers the same emotion repeatedly, creating a cycle of distress and suffering.

Labeling your emotion will help you understand and detach from the situation prompting that emotion, allowing you to achieve a Wise Mind.

THE EMOTIONAL MIND, RATIONAL MIND, AND WISE MIND

The emotional, rational, and wise minds are the three states of mind we operate in. In DBT, the Wise Mind is a core mindfulness skill. By reaching a wise mind, you can attain inner wisdom and intuition. However, to understand how to achieve a wise mind, you must understand what the other two states of mind entail.

Rational Mind

The rational mind is the traditional thinking mind. It's your practical mind responsible for pragmatic, logical, task-oriented, and rule-oriented decision-making rooted in facts and logic.

Emotional Mind

The emotional mind is a direct contrast to the rational mind. It isn't unreasonable, but it depends on emotion rather than reason. This state of mind does not concern itself with facts or logic. In this state of mind, your thinking is governed by your feelings and moods.

You act based on the action urges prompted by your emotional state rather than a carefully curated plan.

Wise mind

Wise mind is a balance of the emotional and rational mind. It's where they both overlap. The wise mind considers both facts and emotions when making a decision. It's practical yet sensitive to our feelings. Reaching the wise mind enables you to behave rationally while staying true to your very nature.

Think about it this way, the two states of mind - rational and emotional - are cold and hot, respectively. Both play crucial roles in thinking and decision-making, but you need to find a balance, i.e., create something warm by reaching the wise mind.

You can achieve this by using the DBT skill of mindfulness and the techniques we discussed in previous chapters. Still, let's look at more techniques to help find this much-needed balance and attain a wise mind.

OPPOSITE ACTION

Emotions alert us to respond, and our responses are biologically wired. You can choose a different response to the default biological response with the Opposite Action skill. For example, thirst alerts you to hydrate, activating an urge to drink water; hunger alerts you to eat, activating an urge to eat; and fatigue alerts you to rest, activating an urge to sleep.

With certain emotions, your best bet is to do the opposite of what your body thinks it should do. For example, when you're afraid, the biological urge you get is to run. But instead, it can help to face your fear. This helps with extreme phobias.

When you're depressed, the body thinks it should shut down and become inactive. But what if you responded by immersing yourself in more physical activities than ever? Then, your mind and body would greatly benefit.

The opposite action skill is beneficial in controlling the natural urges that come with many emotions. Switch up the following emotion by doing the opposite of what they prompt you to do.

Emotion	Biological Urge	Opposite Action
Anger – alerts us to a perceived or real attack.	Activates the urge to attack or defend ourselves.	Walk away, show empathy, kindness, or compassion.
Fear – alerts us to danger.	Activates the urge to hide or run.	Face your fear, build courage, or stay involved in the action.
Shame – prepares us to isolate.	Activates the urge to hide or recoil from a situation.	Maintain eye contact, and raise your head and shoulders.
Depression – tells us to become inactive.	Activates the urge to withdraw and avoid contact.	Become more socially active than ever.
Disgust – alerts us to avoid something.	Activates the urge to reject or avoid yourself.	Motivate yourself and push through the situation.
Guilt – tells us to seek forgiveness.	Activates the urge to repent and repair damages.	Apologize meaningfully and change your behavior.

If you want your emotions to remain the same, continue to listen to your natural biological urges and do what your body tells you to. But if you want to change your emotions and have them stick around, continue repeating the opposite actions recommended above.

For this skill to truly work, you must engage in the opposite action of your natural biological responses. But, more importantly, you must trust that it'll work.

ABC PLEASE

The ABC PLEASE skill teaches you to attend to your physical and emotional needs and those of the people in your life. This skill can increase emotional resilience and decrease sensitivity to unpleasant emotions.

- **A - Accumulate positive experiences**

You'll naturally feel good about your life when you have more positive experiences than negative ones. Likewise, you're more likely to bounce back from adversity when you have many positive experiences to look back on. It's like taking $10 out of a $200 bank account balance. Still, even the slightest setback can make you feel powerful emotions.

So, incorporate a wide range of activities such as camping, rappelling, rock climbing, etc. into your life. These activities can make you experience positive emotions regularly. When you build positive memories through these, you can find joy and strength by looking back on them in the face of adversity.

For an experience to truly count, you have to be mindful. There is no point in accumulating positive experiences if you don't do it mindfully. We're often physically present but mentally/emotionally absent for an event because our mind was elsewhere. Call it back to the present if your mind starts to wander and fully immerse yourself in it. In time, it'll become a habit to focus entirely on anything you're doing.

- **B - Build mastery**

Learn and become proficient at new activities, skills, or hobbies. Building mastery encourages you to do things that you genuinely love and enjoy. When you accumulate a repertoire of activities and hobbies that you excel at, it boosts your self-confidence and regularly reinforces your talents and capabilities.

The best thing is that it gives you something to fall back on if you ever fall prey to anxiety, depression, or boredom.

- **C – Cope ahead**

Coping ahead means preparing yourself for potentially stressful or strenuous events. This could be a work or class presentation, a test, or a job interview. Whatever it is, prepare yourself emotionally and mentally. Think of the steps you can take to do this.

With a job interview, you might want to research standard interview questions, review your work history, and prepare references to draw upon in case you're asked for them.

Coping ahead prepares you for any distressing emotion that might arise from the event you're about to experience.

- **PL – Physical health**

Take care of yourself when you're sick or miserable. Physical health is key to emotional health. Physical illness makes it hard to be at your optimal best, negatively impacting your emotional state. Practice physical self-care techniques to influence your emotional health positively.

- **E – Eating**

Healthy eating is necessary. Lack of proper nutrition makes you stressed, sluggish, and passive. So, opt for foods that will keep you energetic and active throughout the day.

- **A – Avoid**

Avoid using mood-altering substances. Stay away from non-prescribed medication; they usually have a negative impact on physical and emotional health. Prescribed medications are measured, regulated, and managed to balance the chemicals in your body. It doesn't help to self-medicate; you'll most likely end up with emotional dysregulation.

- **S – Sleep**

Get adequate sleep. Restful sleep energizes the body, making it easy to complete daily tasks and regulate your emotions.

Tune in with your body to determine the amount of sleep you need.

- **E – Exercise**

Exercise contributes significantly to physical, emotional, and mental health. It decreases stress, anxiety, depression, and other negative emotions. Many neglect physical exercise because they don't realize how incredibly beneficial it can be. You don't have to do high-intensity exercises - something as simple as a daily run can make all the difference.

POSITIVE SELF-TALK

Self-talk refers to those thoughts that dance around in your head all day. They can be positive or negative. Most times, we engage in negative self-talk without realizing it. Negative self-talk makes you perceive life events as being more stressful than they are. Your self-talk may sabotage your emotional regulation efforts by increasing cortisol production and amplifying stress levels.

Luckily, you can deconstruct negative self-talk and replace them with positive ones. Doing this can relieve stress, boost productivity, and improve self-esteem.

Notice your thinking pattern

Pay attention to how often you think about negative things and how these thoughts affect your experiences. You can try journaling to analyze your everyday thoughts and fish out negative patterns. You can also try these two methods:

- **Stop your thought:** Each time you catch a negative thought in your head, stop that thought by saying "STOP" aloud. It's more powerful when you say it out loud. Plus, that makes you aware of how often you have a specific negative thought.
- **Rubber band snaps:** Go everywhere with a rubber band around your wrist. Every time you catch yourself engaging in negative self-talk, pull the rubber band from your skin and release it - snap! It'll hurt, but it'll also make you constantly aware of your thoughts so you can stop the negative ones in their tracks. Suppose you don't want to experience the consequences of negative thoughts. In that case, you should be more conscious of your thoughts and learn to stop them when they arise.

Replace negative thoughts

An excellent way to stop a bad habit is to replace it with a better habit. For example, once you've identified patterns of self-dialogue, you can change them with the following techniques.

- **Use milder wording:** Change how you talk about pain. Replace "pain" with "discomfort." Pain is much more intense than discomfort. The wordings you use to discuss your pain or suffering can make the experience needlessly intense. Replace words such as "hate" and "anger" with "dislike" and "annoyance," respectively. Say, "I dislike this feeling." not "I hate this feeling."

- **Switch from negative to neutral:** Reframe your assumptions when you find yourself mentally complaining. Don't assume a situation is damaging even when nothing suggests it is. Stop, rethink, and come up with a neutral or positive replacement for any negative thought.
- **Turn self-limiting statements to questions:** "I can't do this" or "I'm not good enough" are examples of self-limiting statements. They increase your stress levels, which makes them particularly damaging. Worse, they discourage you from seeking solutions to a problem. Replace them with "How can I do this?" or "Can I handle this?" and you'll find yourself more productive.

In general, bring more positive energy into your life and routine. If you surround yourself with positivity, your mind will become more optimistic.

PROBLEM-SOLVING

There is an underlying problem behind every emotional trigger. In order to reduce how much a trigger affects you, it's best to solve that problem from a DBT perspective. Once you know that certain situations are potentially problematic for you, work on solving the possible problem before you find yourself in that situation again.

- **Analyze your behavior**

Look back on past situations - what causes you to feel emotionally overwhelmed? Is it something at work, with family, your friends, or kids? Write down the emotions you usually experience in these situations and the behavior they prompt.

- **Reflect on what you can change**

What can you change about situations that trigger distressing emotions and prompt a specific action? Understand that the change you want to make should positively impact your emotional health and immediate overwhelming feeling.

You may not be able to change an internal event. Still, you can work on your internal dialogue during the event. Choose two specific things to try to change during the internal or external event - that could be your thoughts, feelings, or action.

- **Find alternatives**

Now that you know what you need to change, it's time to think of possible alternatives. For example, what would be the perfect replacement for the self-dialogue that happens when your partner arrives late for a date? What can you do differently? Perhaps you need to change the event and take a different approach to your thoughts.

- **Apply this solution**

After you've come up with brilliant alternatives to what you can do to change the unchangeable, choose the best one for your situation and put that into action. Then, actively remind yourself to act in an alternative way or use the alternative self-talk the next time you're in a similar situation. Ultimately, that will change how you respond to the event.

And more importantly, it will solve the underlying problem that triggers the emotion.

JOURNALING

Do you know what Albert Einstein, Charles Darwin, Marie Curie, and Thomas Edison had in common? A journal. Journaling is a form of introspection - a way to communicate and stay in touch with yourself. Keeping a journal of your journey as you navigate using DBT skills to change the way you think, feel, and behave is the best decision you'll ever make regarding improving your emotional and mental health.

Introspection is vital because it helps you find creativity, resilience, and tranquility from within, ultimately improving your performance.

I have tried different formats of journaling. Some were more effective than others. I still use various formats, but my favorite is the LIFE method.

- **L – Learnings:** Write down what you learn about yourself – thoughts, emotions, and actions – each day. Write everything down if you learned something from a book, conversation, podcast, or blog. It reinforces your motivation for personal development.
- **I – Ideas:** Write down every new idea you have. The goal is to nurture your creative imagination, so put it down in your journal, whether it's a nuanced observation or an idea for an invention.
- **F - Feelings:** Write down how you feel throughout each day in your journal. Think of this as keeping an emotional inventory. It'll get easier with practice.
- **E - Experiences:** What did you experience today? Did anything fun or notable happen? Write everything in your journal. I recommend adding a sensory layer to each experience to make it more

meaningful. That way, it doesn't feel like a bland grocery list.

Journaling should be a massive part of your DBT journey. It's the best way to track your progress and make improvements where necessary.

Practical Examples of Emotional Regulation

We are almost at the end of this book. But before you go, let me introduce you to three people who found immense power in regulating their emotions: Dan, Lana, and Chris.

Meet Dan.

Dan met Marie at a college function. You could say it was love at first sight. Dan and Marie were immediately taken in with each other. As soon as they finished college, they decided to get married. Marie loved Dan immensely, but she was skeptical about getting married. They had only been together for a few years, yet it seemed like the number of arguments they had doubled with the number of times they had gone on dates. She didn't want a marriage where she'd spend half of the day arguing over the most trivial stuff.

So, Marie sat down and expressed her feelings to him. Dan wasn't surprised, which surprised Marie. He confessed that he's struggled with this since he was mature enough to be in romantic relationships. Dan had tried everything possible to no success. Still, he promised Marie he would put more effort into changing his predisposition for conflict.

He then discussed his situation with a friend who told him how his cousin had used a book about DBT to learn how to take charge of overwhelming emotions. He promised to help Dan borrow the book, and sure enough, he kept his promise.

In reading the book, Dan learned that he constantly got into arguments with his partners because his parents hadn't modeled emotion regulation and good conflict resolution skills to him.

He poured himself into mastering and applying DBT sub-skills such as STOP, DEAR MAN, TIPP, Opposite Action, and mindfulness into his daily conversations. Soon, he began to notice changes. He was beginning to patiently listen to Marie express her feelings and needs without getting defensive and turning it into one big argument.

He used the DBT skill "STOP" whenever he noticed a conversation getting heated. And when he needed to express his feelings or needs, he used the DEAR MAN skill.

Marie was thrilled with Dan's progress. So, a few months later, they got married in a small gathering of friends and family, excited for the journey ahead!

Now meet Lana.

"Would I ever stop sabotaging myself?"

That was the thought in Lana's head as she left the building of her now former workplace. She had been fired. Yet again. She wondered why she couldn't ever control her urges. It's almost like a compulsion to listen to her impulses, even if it gets her into trouble now and then. She decided that it was time to make a change. After all, she can't afford to get fired once again or sabotage another relationship before it's even begun. It was time for a change.

Lana had been seeing a therapist who had told her she could learn to control her emotions and behavior with DBT or CBT skills - she couldn't remember which one. However, she wasn't sure how to do that, so she went back to the therapist to learn more.

Her therapist affirmed that she could transform her life using DBT, a form of therapy focused on regulating one's emotions. First, she needed to learn to control her emotions and limit impulsive behaviors – simple enough.

Lana started practicing everything she learned in therapy. Her therapist gave her homework and worksheets to complete. She learned different techniques that helped regulate her emotions in tense situations, stopping her from impulsively reacting to them.

Lana was happy. For the first time in her life, it seemed like she could think things through and make decisions based on facts rather than emotion. Just the other day, Lana held her breath and counted from 100 to 1 before calmly asking her date why he was late. Usually, she would have snapped at him and probably stormed out in anger.

Knowing how to regulate her emotions made a significant difference in her life. She felt more powerful than ever, knowing her feelings could no longer hold her captive. Now, she's ready to get into the job market and find a new job that she'll hopefully keep for as long as she wants.

What about CHRIS?

Cris has been at his job for ten years - same position, same cubicle. He believed he loved his job, but it didn't feel like it. These days, it felt like he was performing an obligation every time he got up, dressed, and took the subway to work. There was no excitement - He wanted excitement.

He wanted more from life. He had ideas he wanted to present to his boss – ideas that could shoot him to the pinnacle of his career. But each time he thought about showcasing his ideas, he felt a crippling fear followed by distressing thoughts.

"What if she shuts my ideas down?" "What if they aren't good enough?" "I may not be as brilliant as I think I am." "These ideas would probably fail anyway. So what would be the point of presenting them to my boss?"

Feeling discouraged, he decided to keep his ideas to himself and continued to work his lackluster job. Then, one day, he decided to act. He decided that it was time to face his fear of failure if he hoped to leave the darkness, figure out his long-term goals, and make a new positive plan for the future.

In his search for solutions, he stumbled upon a book about DBT.

The DBT book created a turning point in his life. With what he learned in the book, he was able to regulate the feeling of fear that stopped him from pursuing his goals. He learned to face his fears and found power in regulating uncomfortable emotions. Perhaps the best thing the book taught him was how to determine his goals and plan toward them while keeping potential obstructions in check.

He was excited about his future. For the first time in his life, the future held no uncertainties. He knew exactly what he wanted to do and how he wanted to do it.

"Nothing could go wrong. I am master of my emotions and in control of my own life now," he said aloud as he walked into his boss' office to present his ideas.

CONCLUSION

Great job!

You're now at the end of your journey with me, and I must commend you for staying with me to this point. It's been an exciting experience for me, and I hope it was for you as well.

I hope you've learned the invaluable skills of DBT that will help you make positive changes in your life. You're ready to utilize them to end your battle with anxiety, calm your raging emotions, and achieve mental wellness. No doubt, we all want a life without pain and one free of overwhelming emotions, but the question is, are you ready to do the work that will get you closer to your wishes?

I've discussed what DBT entails and the four essential skills of DBT. I discussed the different benefits mindfulness offers you and how you can use techniques like mindful eating, mindful breathing, mindful walking, and body scans to stay in the present moment and calm your emotions.

As humans, we'll likely experience extreme emotional states at some point, which is where distress tolerance comes in. With techniques such as IMPROVE, ACCEPTS, TIPP, self-soothing, radical acceptance, and distractions, you can easily handle difficult emotions and quickly return to a calm state when you encounter stressors.

Sometimes, you can have tense interactions with your family, friends, or co-workers, complicating your relationship with them. I discussed strategies such as GIVE, FAST, DEAR MAN, THINK, and other tips to help you improve your social skills.

In the book's final chapters, we discussed the power of regulating our impulses, fears, anger, mood swings, chronic boredom, and self-image using the five critical aspects of emotional intelligence and other DBT techniques (journaling, ABC PLEASE, opposite action, and positive self-talk.

Even though the skills and techniques of DBT are separate, combined practices will lead to a life worth living.

You may encounter challenges as you strive to become better and live a happier life. However, I believe you won't give up or let your hard work go to waste. Get back up and keep moving because your reward is closer then you think.

I've always been passionate about this topic because I understand the pain that comes with intense emotions and behaviors. When it came down to it, putting these newfound skills into practice consistently is what changed my life for the better! After six months of consistent practice, I had more control over my emotions, and people around me started noticing.

I am happy that I have the opportunity to share this information that has liberated many people in the same rut as you. This book is my special gift to you, and I hope you heal from whatever kind of pain you feel and find peace.

There isn't a hard and fast rule here when it comes to getting started. There are techniques and strategies you will feel more comfortable with and relate to them more easily. You can start with those and commit to them; you will gradually explore others. This book is always here for you to revisit and apply the techniques when needed.

Are you ready to launch into a new phase where you'll live a happier and fulfilled life? I think I got a resounding YES from you.

Everyone deserves the right to a life worth living. While reviews are important to me, it's more important that other people with the same experience as us have the opportunity to read reviews and get the help they need.

Best wishes!

REFERENCES

Ackerman, C. (December, 2017). *Interpersonal Effectiveness: 9 Worksheets & Examples (+ PDF).* Retrieved from Positive Psychology https://positivepsychology.com/interpersonal-effectiveness/#dbt-interpersonal-effectiveness

Allied Services Integrated Health System. (June, 2020). *The vagus nerve: your secret weapon in fighting stress.* Retrieved from Allied Services https://www.allied-services.org/news/2020/june/the-vagus-nerve-your-secret-weapon-in-fighting-s/

Barnes, S., Brown, K. W., Krusemark, E., Campbell, W. K., & Rogge, R. D. (2007). *The role of mindfulness in romantic relationship satisfaction and responses to relationship stress. Journal of marital and family therapy.* Retrieved from https://doi.org/10.1111/j.1752-0606.2007.00033.x

Brownne, S.J. (April, 2021). *What The Vagus Nerve Is And How To Stimulate It For Better Mental Health.* Retrieved from Forbes https://www.forbes.com/sites/womensmedia/2021/04/15/what-the-vagus-nerve-is-and-how-to-stimulate-it-for-better-mental-health/?sh=6d9a83236250

Caballo, V et al. (2014). *Assessing social skills: the factorial structure and other psychometric properties of four self-report measures.* ResearchGate https://www.researchgate.net/publication/269519251_Assessing_social_skills_the_factorial_structure_and_other_psychometric_properties_of_four_self-report_measures/citation/download

CBT Los Angeles. (n.d). *Mindfulness from a DBT Perspective.* Retrieved from CBT L.A https://cogbtherapy.com/cbt-blog/mindfulness-in-dbt

Chambers, R., Lo, B. C. Y., & Allen, N. B. (2008). *The impact of intensive mindfulness training on attentional control, cognitive style, and affect. Cognitive Therapy and Research.* Retrieved from https://doi.org/10.1007/s10608-007-9119-0

Cherry, K. (January, 2022). *5 Key Emotional Intelligence Skills.* Retrieved from Verywell Mind https://www.verywellmind.com/components-of-emotional-intelligence-2795438

Cleveland Clinic. (n.d). *Dialectical Behavior Therapy (DBT).* Retrieved from

Cleveland Clinic https://my.clevelandclinic.org/health/treatments/22838-dialectical-behavior-therapy-dbt

CACI Research & Education. (October, 2018). *Probiotics and the Vagus Nerve – a New Frontier for Psychiatric Conditions.* Retrieved from CASI https://blog.designsforhealth.com/node/892

Daphne, M.D & Jeffrey, A. (July, 2012). *What are the benefits of mindfulness?* Retrieved from American Psychological Association. https://www.apa.org/monitor/2012/07-08/ce-corner

DBT Selfhelp. (n.d). *Factors Reducing Interpersonal Effectiveness.* Retrieved from DBT Selfhelp https://dbtselfhelp.com/dbt-skills-list/interpersonal-effectiveness/factors-reducing-interpersonal-effectiveness/

DBT Selfhelp. (n.d). *Identifying & Describing Emotions.* Retrieved from DBT Selfhelp https://dbtselfhelp.com/dbt-skills-list/emotion-regulation/identifying-describing-emotions/

DBT Selfhelp. (n.d). *Objectives Effectiveness: DEAR MAN.* Retrieved from DBT Selfhelp https://dbtselfhelp.com/dbt-skills-list/interpersonal-effectiveness/dear-man/

DBT Selfhelp. (n.d). *Relationship Effectiveness: GIVE.* Retrieved from DBT Selfhelp https://dbtselfhelp.com/dbt-skills-list/interpersonal-effectiveness/give/

DBT Selfhelp. (n.d). *Self-Soothe.* Retrieved from DBT Selfhelp https://dbtselfhelp.com/dbt-skills-list/distress-tolerance/self-soothe/

DBT Selfhelp. (n.d). *Self-Respect Effectiveness: FAST.* Retrieved DBT Selfhelp https://dbtselfhelp.com/dbt-skills-list/interpersonal-effectiveness/fast/

EHN Canada. (October, 2021). *The Seven Pillars of Mindfulness.* Retrieved from EHN Resources https://www.edgewoodhealthnetwork.com/resources/blog/the-seven-pillars-of-mindfulness/

Fossas, A. (January, 2015). *The Basics of Mindfulness: Where Did It Come From?* Retrieved from Welldoing.org https://welldoing.org/article/basics-of-mindfulness-come-from

Giang, C.H. (n.d). *What Are The Origins Of Mindfulness?* Retrieved from Thrive Global https://thriveglobal.com/stories/what-are-the-origins-of-mindfulness/

Gelles, D. (n.d). *How to Meditate.* Retrieved from New York Times https://www.nytimes.com/guides/well/how-to-meditate

Gross, J. (September, 1998).The Emerging Field of Emotion Regulation: An

Integrative Review. Retrieved from Sage Journals https://doi.org/10.1037/1089-2680.2.3.271

Han, S. (April, 2020). *Your Parasympathetic Nervous System Explained.* Retrieved from Healthline https://www.healthline.com/health/parasympathetic-nervous-system

Harris, A. (June, 2020). *Radical Acceptance in a Time of Uncertainty*. Retrieved from HopeWay https://hopeway.org/blog/radical-acceptance

Headway Clinic. (n.d). *What is DBT?* Retrieved from Headway Clinic https://www.headwayclinic.ca/what-is-dbt/

Hofmann, S. G., Sawyer, A. T., Witt, A. A., & Oh, D. (2010). *The effect of mindfulness-based therapy on anxiety and depression: A meta-analytic review. Journal of consulting and clinical psychology.* Retrieved from https://doi.org/10.1037/a0018555

Juul, L., Pallesen, K. J., Piet, J., Parsons, C., & Fjorback, L. O. (2018). *Effectiveness of Mindfulness-Based Stress Reduction in a Self-Selecting and Self-Paying Community Setting. Mindfulness, 9(4), 1288–1298.* https://doi.org/10.1007/s12671-017-0873-0

Keng, S. L., Smoski, M. J., & Robins, C. J. (2011). *Effects of mindfulness on psychological health: a review of empirical studies. Clinical psychology review, 31(6), 1041–1056.* https://doi.org/10.1016/j.cpr.2011.04.006

Mayo Clinic. (n.d). *Stress management.* Retrieved from Mayo Clinic https://www.mayoclinic.org/healthy-lifestyle/stress-management/in-depth/stress/art-20046037

National Wellness Institute. (n.d). *Understanding Emotional Triggers.* Retrieevd from NWI https://www.ab.bluecross.ca/pdfs/workplace-wellness-resources/Emotional-Triggers-Tool.pdf

M1 Psychology. (n.d). *Developing Emotional Awareness.* Retrieved from M1 Psychology https://m1psychology.com/developing-emotional-awareness/

Osea Malibu. (n.d). *Massage for Vagus Nerve Stimulation.* Retrieved from Osea Malibu https://oseamalibu.com/blogs/wellness-blog/massage-for-vagus-nerve-stimulation

Ortner, Catherine & Kilner, Sachne & Zelazo, Philip. (2007). *Mindfulness meditation and reduced emotional interference on a cognitive task. Motivation and Emotion.* Retrieved from Research Gate https://www.researchgate.net/publication/

226504935_Mindfulness_meditation_and_reduced_emotional_interference_on_a_cognitive_task

Psychological Care & Healing Center. (n.d). *Emotional Dysregulation.* Retrieved from PCH https://www.pchtreatment.com/who-we-treat/emotional-dysregulation/

Robertson, R. (August, 2022). *The Gut-Brain Connection: How it Works and The Role of Nutrition.* Retrieved from Healthline https://www.healthline.com/nutrition/gut-brain-connection#TOC_TITLE_HDR_3

Schimelpfening, N. (July, 2022). *What Is Dialectical Behavior Therapy (DBT)?* Retrieved from Verywell Mind https://www.verywellmind.com/dialectical-behavior-therapy-1067402

Sunrise RTC. (n.d). *DBT Interpersonal Effectiveness Skills: The Guide to Healthy Relationships.* Retrieved from Sunrise https://sunrisertc.com/interpersonal-effectiveness/

Tull, V. (July, 2020). *What Is Distress Tolerance?* Retrieved from Verywell Mind https://www.verywellmind.com/distress-tolerance-2797294

Vaughn, S. (October, 2021). *History of DBT: Origins and Foundations.* Retrieved from Psychotherapy Academy https://psychotherapyacademy.org/dbt/history-of-dialectical-behavioral-therapy-a-very-brief-introduction/

Vay, K. (n.d). *What is DBT and How Does It Differ from Other Treatment?* Retrieved from Impact Parent https://impactparents.com/blog/anxiety/what-is-dbt-and-how-does-it-differ-from-other-treatment/

www.ingramcontent.com/pod-product-compliance
Lightning Source LLC
LaVergne TN
LVHW052327200926
848481LV00002B/690